South African Business in China

Sino-African relations have evoked a great deal of geo-strategic interest in recent years. Most attention has focused on China's assistance to and growing involvement in the economic development of several African nations. Far less emphasis has been placed on Africans in China and on African actors' involvement over the Chinese economy, despite the importance of both to genuinely bilateral economic relations.

This is one of the first studies to focus on South African foreign direct investment (FDI) in Mainland China. The research aims to identify and specify the key institutional factors that have contributed to the effectiveness or otherwise of South African firms entering and operating within the Chinese market. The research also investigates the characteristics and processes that have effectively shaped South African firms' business strategies to negotiate the current Chinese institutional environment. The study's primary empirical contribution is ten real-life case studies drawn from a cross section of South African business actors who have sought to penetrate the Chinese market. These case studies are interrogated conceptually by means of a three-dimensional institutional model, which explores the role of formal and informal business processes and practices in influencing business success and failure in the Sino-South African context.

It will be of value to researchers, academics, policymakers, Sino-African business practitioners and advanced students in the fields of international business, political economy, strategy and Asian and African studies.

Dr. Kelly Meng is Programme Director and Lecturer for the MA Luxury Brand Management Program at Goldsmiths, University of London, UK.

Routledge Focus on Business and Management

The fields of business and management have grown exponentially as areas of research and education. This growth presents challenges for readers trying to keep up with the latest important insights. *Routledge Focus on Business and Management* presents small books on big topics and how they intersect with the world of business research.

Individually, each title in the series provides coverage of a key academic topic, whilst collectively, the series forms a comprehensive collection across the business disciplines.

Corporate Governance Models
A Critical Assessment
Marco Mastrodascio

Continuous Improvement Practice in Local Government
Insights from Australia and New Zealand
Matthew Pepper, Oriana Price and Arun Elias

Informal Leadership, Strategy and Organizational Change
The Power of Silent Authority
Brenetia J. Adams-Robinson

South African Business in China
Navigating Institutions
Kelly Meng

Privatisation in India
Journey and Challenges
Sudhir Naib

For more information about this series, please visit: www.routledge.com/
Routledge-Focus-on-Business-and-Management/book-series/FBM

South African Business in China

Navigating Institutions

Kelly Meng

Routledge
Taylor & Francis Group

NEW YORK AND LONDON

First published 2022
by Routledge
605 Third Avenue, New York, NY 10158

and by Routledge
4 Park Square, Milton Park, Abingdon, Oxon, OX14 4RN

Routledge is an imprint of the Taylor & Francis Group, an informa business

© 2022 Kelly Meng

Library of Congress Cataloging-in-Publication Data
Names: Meng, Kelly, 1982– author.
Title: South African business in China : navigating institutions /
    Dr. Kelly Meng.
Description: New York, NY : Routledge, 2022. | Series: Routledge focus on
    business and management | Includes bibliographical references and index.
Identifiers: LCCN 2021047802 (print) | LCCN 2021047803 (ebook) |
    ISBN 9780367761301 (hardback) | ISBN 9780367761417 (paperback) |
    ISBN 9781003165668 (ebook)
Subjects: LCSH: South Africa—Commerce—China—Case studies. |
    China—Commerce—South Africa—Case studies.
Classification: LCC HF3901.Z7 C664 2022 (print) | LCC HF3901.Z7
    (ebook) | DDC 382.0968/051—dc23/eng/20211001
LC record available at https://lccn.loc.gov/2021047802
LC ebook record available at https://lccn.loc.gov/2021047803

ISBN: 978-0-367-76130-1 (hbk)
ISBN: 978-0-367-76141-7 (pbk)
ISBN: 978-1-003-16566-8 (ebk)

DOI: 10.4324/9781003165668

Typeset in Times New Roman
by Apex CoVantage, LLC

Contents

Preface   viii

1   An Introduction   1

     1.1   The Early History of Relations Between China and Africa   1
     1.2   The Modern Development of Sino-African Relations   6
         The Early Cold War Era (1950s to the Mid-1970s)   6
         The Transitional Era (Mid-1970s to the 1990s)   8
         The Sino-Africa New Age (the Twenty-First Century)   9
     1.3   China and South African Political and Economic Relations: An Institutional Transition View   11
         Introduction: South Africa and China's Comparative Transitions   11
         Constriction to Autonomy (1866 to 1948)   15
             South Africa: Late British Colonial Era and the Mineral Revolution   15
             China: Journey From an Empire to a Republic   17
         Self-Reliance and International Re-Connection (1948 to 1994)   17
             South Africa – Apartheid Regime   17
             China: From Planned Economy to Open-Door Policy (1949–1994)   19

*Globalisation and South-South Cooperation
(1994 to Present) 21*
South Africa: The Post-Apartheid Era 21
*China: Open Doors and Unprecedented
Development 22*

2   Institutional Environments and an Institutional Model   27

*2.1 An Institutional Perspective in International
Business Studies 28*
A Brief Introduction 28
The Institutional Approach in IB Studies 30
*Institutions Operationalised: Applying an
Institutional Approach to This Study 33*
*2.2 The Chinese Institutional Environment for
South African Investment 36*
2.2.1 Formal Institutions in China 37
Macro-Level Institutions 37
Meso-Level Institutions 41
Micro-Level Institutions 41
2.2.2 Informal Institutions in China 44
What Is Guanxi? 44
Where Does Guanxi Come From? 45
How Important Is Guanxi? 47
How Is Guanxi Institutionalised? 48
Guanxi and Foreign Firms *50*
2.3 A Three-Dimensional (3D) Institutional Model 52

3   Case Studies and 3D Institutional Model Analysis   57

3.1 A Fine Line Between Success and Failure 57
Analysis of Company A's *Chinese Business Strategies
Within the 3D Institutional Model 59*
Analysis of Company B's *Chinese Business Strategies
Within the 3D Institutional Model 63*
*3.2 Financial Market: Different Targets, Different
Strategies and Different Outcomes 65*
Analysis of Company C's *Chinese Business Strategies
Within the 3D Institutional Model 66*

Analysis of Company D's *Chinese Business Strategies Under the 3D Institutional Model 70*

Analysis of Company E's *Chinese Business Strategies Under the 3D Institutional Model 73*

Analysis of Company F's *Chinese Business Strategies Under the 3D Institutional Model 77*

3.3 *Machinery Market: Business Partners Control the Fate of the Business 79*

Analysis of Company G's *Chinese Business Strategies Under the 3D Institutional Model 79*

Analysis of Company H's *Chinese Business Strategies Under the 3D Institutional Model 84*

3.4 *Energy Sector: Business Sometimes Comes Second; Relationship With the Government Is Key 87*

Analysis of Company I's *Chinese Business Strategies Under the 3D Institutional Model 89*

Analysis of Company J's *Chinese Business Strategies Under the 3D Institutional Model 94*

4 Conclusion   **98**

4.1 *Key Findings 98*

4.2 *A South African Business Flavour? 101*

4.3 *Contributions to the Study of International Business 104*

4.4 *Suggestions for Further Research 106*

References   108
Index   119

Preface

When I completed my PhD back in 2014, I was unable to publish my research immediately due to confidentiality commitments that I gave to my various research participants. Now that a suitable and acceptable period of time has elapsed, I am presenting the theoretical and empirical material from my research in the hope that it will contribute an insightful understanding of how some of the pioneer South African firms entered the Chinese market and consolidated their operations there.

This book aims to make a timely contribution to the evolving and important field of Sino-African relations, and is one of the first pieces of research to look at the Africa-to-China directionality of economic interaction. The focus is on the business strategies adopted by South African firms as they seek to penetrate and become established within the Mainland Chinese markets. Using originally composed real-life case studies, the book demonstrates how South African firms navigate sometimes complicated formal and informal institutional environments in order to gain a foothold in China. The book's empirical findings are of considerable potential interest to business and policy-making practitioners across the African continent, whilst the original conceptual tools which are developed to interrogate the primary research findings will be of interest and value to the academic community. A further strength of the book is its multi-disciplinary character, drawing on the fields of International Business and International Political Economy, as well as Asian and African Area Studies.

Sino-African relations have evoked a great deal of geo-strategic interest in recent years. Most attention has focused on China's assistance to and growing involvement in the economic development of several African nations. Far less emphasis has been placed on Africans in China and on African actors' involvement over the Chinese economy, despite the importance of both to genuinely bilateral economic relations. It is widely accepted that entry into and consolidation within the Chinese market is challenging to many foreign firms, not least because of linguistic, cultural, political and institutional hurdles. Such obstacles are even more daunting for actors from countries which have only limited historical connections with China, including many in sub-Saharan Africa.

Despite being one of the world's important emerging economies and a growing international economic player, as well as the only African member of the G20, most international academic attention on South Africa has tended to focus on political issues, which have tended to overshadow critical analysis from an international business perspective. Certainly, from an investment point of view, South Africa has not hitherto received the same level of research focus on foreign direct investment (FDI) flows to and from other emerging economies as has been the case for most advanced economies. The Chinese market has become an increasingly important focus for outward FDI from the Republic of South Africa, possibly leading the way for other African nations to follow, but hitherto there has been very little primary research interest in these investment flows. The book presents research findings from in-depth investigations of ten South African firms (approximately one-third of all South African firms that became established in the Chinese markets after the year 2000) across several economic sectors, and consisting of both successful and less-successful business outcomes.

The primary research upon which this book is based explores how business actors from one of Africa's leading economies, South Africa, have developed strategies to gain access to the Chinese market, some more successfully than others. The key focus is on how they engaged with and navigated a path through the Chinese social, cultural, political and regulatory environments, manifest in various sets of formal and informal institutions and associated practices. In order to structure this empirical investigation, a three-dimensional institutional model is developed which emphasises the macro-, meso- and micro-level institutions that business actors must negotiate in China, the formal and informal processes in which they must engage (typically a combination of both) and the factors that are both external (generic) and internal (firm-specific) to business negotiations that actors have to accommodate.

The book contains an admixture of theoretical and empirical components, which should appeal to students in various disciplinary fields who take an interest in international business, and in both Africa and China. The arrangement of the book's contents is coherent, but it is designed in such a way that each chapter of the book can be used independently. That is to say, students, business practitioners and policy-makers who are interested in the empirical material, and on the Area Studies elements, can focus in particular on the case studies in Chapter Three, whereas those of a more scholarly persuasion may be drawn in particular to the institutional model in Chapter Two. The book is nonetheless principally beneficial to a readership who will take its two principal components in tandem. Ultimately, for International Business Studies, studying classic business cases is an effective way to engage with theory and apply this to real business situations. So, the value of studying the case studies is not simply to engage fresh data, but it also rests on the strategic and cognitive insight one can obtain by interrogating insightful case histories.

1 An Introduction

1.1 The Early History of Relations Between China and Africa

For many Chinese, the fifth of the Seven Voyages of Admiral Zheng He[1] would popularly be understood as the first formal connection between China and the continent of Africa (Dreyer, 2006), which is the official narrative that many of us learn at school. But in fact Zheng He's epic voyages, which eventually reached the Horn of Africa and the Swahili Coast, followed established routes and were based on sea-faring, cartographic and first-hand geographic knowledge gained from maritime trade and tributary missions that preceded Zheng He's journeys by centuries (Chang, 1974). What follows is a brief sketch of early historical connections between China and Africa.

There is documentary and archaeological evidence that the first indirect connections between China and Africa can be traced to the Chinese Han Dynasty (202 BC–220 AD), or even earlier, based on archaeological finds of silk and other commodity objects discovered in Egypt and Ethiopia (Li, 2015a, 36–37) and Somalia and Zanzibar (Chang, 1974, 352). Early travellers, such as King Mu (975–922 BC) of the Zhou Dynasty (1046–256 BC), who is believed to have travelled the Silk Road around 959 BC, and the imperial envoy, Zhang Qian (164–114 BC), who undertook official missions on behalf of the Han Emperor Wu Di to the western regions between 138 and 115 BC, were important early Chinese sources of official information about the lands, peoples, cultures and trading networks beyond Central Asia, including the Red Sea (Yang, 2009, 19). Zhang Qian mentions reaching a place named Likan, which some analysts claimed was Alexandria in Egypt (Gao, 1984, 241). In 97 BC Gan Ying was sent on an official mission to the Roman Empire (Daqin) and, although unable to reach Rome, he arrived at the 'western sea', which is believed to be the Persian Gulf (Lin, 2004, 327) and just possibly the Eritrean coast (Smidt, 2001), where he observed the importance of trade between the Mediterranean, the Red Sea,

DOI: 10.4324/9781003165668-1

the Persian Gulf and India along a burgeoning southern sea route, which was beginning to supersede the land-based caravan trade (Young, 2001). Whilst these early official travellers are unlikely to have reached the coastal states of Africa, Professor Anshan Li, in his seminal book *The Overseas Chinese in Africa* (2000, 2012a) contends, based on archival and archaeological evidence, both explicit and implicit, that initial contacts between China and Africa had already taken place among private actors. Furthermore, trade routes between Africa and China were beginning to consolidate: Indian merchants were trading with the Aksumite Kingdom in present-day Ethiopia and Eritrea, as evidenced by finds of ancient Indian coins in the Adulis coast (Eritrea), and merchants from the Red Sea were also present in India and Ceylon, where they came into contact with traders and travellers from China (Smidt, 2001).

By and large Indian and Middle Eastern traders were the principal conduits of information to China about the western seas and territories until the middle of the Eighth Century when Du Huan is believed to have been the first Chinese to have visited Africa via the Abbasid Caliphate, which was centred on Baghdad but included most of the Middle East and the northern Red Sea and southern Mediterranean coasts. Du Huan was captured during the Battle of Talas[2] in 751 AD and taken west where he had the opportunity to travel extensively throughout the caliphate. His *Jingxingji* (or travel tales) provided a great deal of information on the lives and cultures of the peoples of the region, and whilst he may not have directly visited all of the areas to which he refers in his travel record, he mentions travelling to Molin which appears to have been located somewhere in the region of present-day Sudan or Eritrea (Smidt, 2001), or perhaps as far south as Kenya (Gao, 1984, 243). Already by the late Eighth Century detailed maps of the 'western regions' had been produced, along with the principal land and sea routes (Chang, 1974, 155).

After Du Huan's visit, direct connections between China and Africa had steadily increased during the later Tang Dynasty (618–907) and as international commerce grew, merchants gained in status and the government relied increasingly on customs revenue (Finlay, 2008, 331), even though only a limited number of Chinese actually travelled to Africa, and Chinese merchant boats had not yet landed on the African continent (Li, 2000). Persian and Arab merchants were the principal intermediary agents for Sino-African trade (Schottenhammer, 2016, 137), with a large Persian community developing in Guangzhou during the Ninth Century (Chaffee, 2018). Chinese porcelain was the principal commodity being traded with the African Red Sea states and eastern Africa (Chang, 1974, 147; Li, 2000, 2012a). Maritime trade, diplomatic and independent connections between China and Africa intensified and became more formalised during the four hundred years of the Song (960–1279) and Yuan (1279–1368) dynasties

(Li, 2000), most particularly after 1127 when China's access to Central Asia was severed in the northwest by Jin Dynasty conquerors, which shifted the focus significantly towards maritime routes (Finlay, 2008, 331). By the time of Zheng He's fifth voyage in 1417, the first to reach Africa, China's carto- graphic knowledge of the near continent was already quite detailed: Four- teenth Century maps reflected the shape of the continent quite accurately, showing the location of the Sahara Desert (Gao, 1984, 244), the correct position and orientation of the Nile and Congo Rivers, as well as the Orange River in today's South Africa (Chang, 1974, 352; see also Chang, 1970).

Zheng He was tasked by Emperor Yong-le to utilise China's technological skills in boat-building and navigation to venture into and beyond the known worlds of South-East Asia, the Indian Ocean and the Middle East with the dual aims of engaging tributary allies and spreading Chinese prestige in these areas (Sen, 2016, 632). Zheng He's voyages are variously described as "the expansion of the Middle Kingdom by [means of] friendly trade and alli- ance" (Peterson, 1994, 43) or a form of proto-colonialism intended to estab- lish a '*pax* Ming' (Wade, 2005). A further objective was to bring maritime trade under government control and to establish direct (and perhaps coer- cive) lines of connection with tributary states (Finlay, 2008, 336). Certainly, the scale of Zeng He's fleet – some 300 vessels, many larger than had ever previously sailed the Indian Ocean, and 28,000 men, many of whom were soldiers – was spectacular and unprecedented (Finlay, 2008, 330). Zheng He's fleet is believed to have visited eastern Africa (principally Somalia and Kenya) on two or three occasions (Alden and Alves, 2008, 46). From the fourth voyage onwards, envoys from eastern Africa were among many who were taken back to China to pay tribute to Emperor Yong-le, thereby estab- lishing their vassal status to the Middle Kingdom. Zheng He's fleet also car- ried commodities to exchange for local products, which helps to explain how porcelain of the Ming Dynasty has been found in African locations as diverse as Egypt, the Sudan, Somalia, Ethiopia, Kenya, Tanganyika, Madagascar, Zimbabwe and the Transvaal of South Africa (Gao, 1984, 245).

Following Zheng He's seventh and last voyage, China's pre-eminent posi- tion as a powerful and dominant maritime force quickly went into decline, in parallel to the declivity of the Ming Dynasty itself. A return to traditional Confucian values, which proscribed trade for profit, led to the prohibition of private overseas trade (something that had been proposed by the Hongwu emperor in 1390 before Yong-le's period of adventurism and militarism), which was only partially lifted in 1567 (Finlay, 2008, 338–339), by which time the Europeans had already started making inroads into the trade and territories of the South China Sea. China's self-imposed isolationism dur- ing the late-Ming significantly curtailed not only its involvement in foreign affairs but also its control of maritime trade, much of which returned to private hands, albeit illicitly. By the time of the Qing Dynasty (1644–1912), Sino-African relations had almost turned full circle: formal diplomatic relations between the two regions were severed, although private interactions continued; direct trade was replaced by indirect commercial ties (Li, 2015b).

An important dimension to the growing connectivity of China and Africa from the Tang Dynasty onwards was the arrival of African people on Chinese soil, and much later the movement of large numbers of Chinese people to, in particular, South Africa. Many Africans were brought to China by Arab merchant ships, mainly as slaves and servants (Gao, 1984, 243), including to the large Arab community living in Guangzhou, but some also "served as soldiers or military leaders, royal guards, government officials, traders, artists, animal trainers and labourers in ancient China" (Li, 2015b, 19). Finlay (2008, 332) refers to 'African stewards' manning the junks of Chinese entrepreneurs that plied the Indian Ocean during the Yuan Dynasty, as Chinese merchants took over seaborne commerce from the Indians and Persians. Zheng He brought non-slave emissaries to China from the East African coast during his fifth voyage in 1417–1419, and one of the reasons for the delayed seventh voyage was to return these emissaries to their home countries. There was a significant increase in the number of black slaves brought to China from Africa after the Portuguese established a trade connection with China in 1535 and a settlement in Macau from 1563 (Wyatt, 2010). Most of these slaves were brought from the western coasts of Africa and were victims of the then-burgeoning Atlantic slave trade. By the mid-Seventeenth Century, Wyatt (2010) claims there were some 5,000 mostly African slaves in Macau, compared to only 2,000 Portuguese settlers.

In the opposite direction, the first major flow of Chinese to South Africa occurred in 1904, when some 63,695 indentured labourers were recruited to work in the gold fields of the Witwatersrand Basin in the Transvaal (formerly Zuid-Afrikaansche Republiek) (Richardson, 1977). Severe labour shortages followed the conclusion of the second Anglo-Boer War of 1899–1902, as African workers drawn from neighbouring Portuguese East Africa (Moçambique) started to desert the mines and return home because of low wages and poor working conditions (Richardson, 1977, 91–92; Meyer and Steyn, 2016), and yet the gold-mining industry was crucial to economic recovery following the disruption and deprivations of the war. A fixed international price for gold, set against the generally poor quality of the Witwatersrand gold ore and capital flight from South Africa during the Boer War, determined that increased production through mechanisation was not a realistic option (Richardson, 1977, 88), and thus a source of labourers to work in the deep mines was urgently needed to return the gold fields to profitability. By the early Twentieth Century, organised international labour migration had become an established means of easing labour shortages in colonial territories, not least by the British who had taken Indians to East Africa in the 1890s and whose liberal immigration policies in Southeast Asia had seen millions of mostly southern Chinese emigrate to the region (Niew, 1969). Before the 1860s, the Chinese Imperial Government had largely prohibited emigration, but in 1860 it signed a convention with the British and French permitting Chinese citizens to emigrate to work in their respective colonies. In 1904 the British and Chinese signed the Emigration Convention Between the United Kingdom and China Respecting the Employment of Chinese Labour in the British Colonies and Protectorates (Niew, 1969, 47), and this agreement allowed the movement of large numbers of indentured labourers to South Africa.

The arrangement was mutually beneficial: South Africa was able significantly to ease labour constraints in the mining sector by importing cheap and hard-working labourers, first from southern China and later from the north and northeast; Chinese people, on the other hand, were able to escape poverty, un- and under-employment, floods, droughts, famine and the effects of the Boxer Rebellion in 1900 to obtain gainful employment abroad (Niew, 1969, 43). The labour movements were organised and formalised with a high degree of state participation (Richardson, 1977, 85) involving the Chamber of Mines Labour Importation Agency, as well as the Chamber of Commerce and the Legislative Council of South Africa. Chinese workers were indentured, under the Labour Importation Ordinance, for a period of three years, extendable to five, to be followed by compulsory repatriation to China. They had to work for ten hours a day, six days a week, typically in the deep mines, for a remuneration of a shilling a day for the first six months, and thereafter 50 shillings per month (Kynoch, 2003, 319). The cost of bringing each labourer to South Africa from China averaged £17 5s 2d (Richardson, 1977, 93). Conditions for Chinese workers were harsh, leading to frequent conflicts and riots, but an indentured labourer could only terminate their contract by reimbursing the full cost of transportation – effectively a full 9–10 months of earnings.

Subsequent waves of Chinese migration to South Africa occurred in the mid-1980s when the Republic was under strict economic sanctions by the international community as a result of its Apartheid policy. These Chinese people were referred to as 'Taiwanese', as Taiwan was one of few countries/regions to maintain diplomatic relations with South Africa during this time. The white South African government attracted a large number of Taiwanese entrepreneurs to set up factories in South Africa (mainly in the textile industry) with generous government subsidies. It is estimated that the total number of Taiwanese in South Africa once reached more than 30,000, but currently there are only about 6,000. A third wave of mainland Chinese immigration started in the early 1990s. At present, it is estimated that between 400,000 and 500,000 Chinese live in South Africa, of which Fujianese make up the highest percentage.

Each occasion of mass Chinese emigration to South Africa evokes significant political, economic as well as social impacts on business relations between the two nations and this will be the focus of our discussion in the following section.

1.2   The Modern Development of Sino-African Relations

In the previous section, we stated that diplomatic relations between China and some African countries ground to a halt during the late Ming Dynasty and there was only little change in that throughout the Qing Dynasty (1644–1912). Although interpersonal connections continued between people from the two regions, bilateral ties between China and Africa largely stagnated during the period of European colonial dominance. It was not until 1949 when the Communist Party of China (CPC) came to power that the People's Republic of China, as an independent and sovereign nation, engaged directly with Africa for the first time in the Twentieth Century. In the following paragraphs we will divide modern Sino-African relations into three periods to highlight the key events and developments in the interactions between China and Africa during the last 70 years: a chronology that many scholars of Sino-African studies tend to follow (Konings, 2007; Stahl, 2016).

The Early Cold War Era (1950s to the Mid-1970s)

The milestone that signified China's re-connection with Africa after decades of formal institutional distance was the Bandung Conference in April 1955, which was the first major meeting of African and Asian states to take place during the post-colonial era. The PRC's (People's Republic of China's) participation in the Conference also marked a significant shift in foreign policy focus, beyond its original preoccupation with the neighbouring states of Asia towards the so-called 'Third World' (Tomlinson, 2003, 309).[3] There were clear and overt strategic objectives behind China's subsequent intensified engagement with Africa (Yu, 1988, 850–851; Hutchinson, 1975): the collective struggle of the world's poorer countries to get rid themselves of the shackles of colonialism, imperialism and underdevelopment offered Communist China a dynamic arena in which it was able to project its revolutionary ideology and create a 'third force' in international politics; and winning friends in Africa was seen as an essential precursor to gaining international recognition for the PRC as the single and sole representative of China, including a seat in the UN General Assembly, at the cost of Taiwan (Republic of China),[4] which hitherto had been very successful in gaining favour in Africa.

A year after the Bandung Conference, Egypt (one of six African attendees) became the first African nation formally to establish diplomatic relations with China, followed by four mostly northern African states (Morocco, Algeria, Sudan and Guinea) in the late 1950s. Diplomatic efforts intensified considerably with three visits of Chinese Premier Zhou En'lai to ten African countries between 1963 and 1965. Further influence was leveraged through aid and development assistance to African states, which mostly focused on the agricultural, light industrial and mining sectors with an emphasis on satisfying the basic needs of local populations. The Chinese referred to this aid as "the poor helping the poor" (Chin and Frolic, 2007, 4): China's GDP per capita in 1964 was only $85.5, compared with $162.6 in Egypt and $230.1 in Ghana (data.worldbank.org, accessed 9 August 2021). Development assistance followed the 'Eight Principles of Economic and Technical Aid' that had been announced by Zhou En'Lai during his visit to Ghana in 1964: these included equality and mutual benefit; respect for sovereignty and no conditionality; interest-free or no-interest loans; assistance to gain independence and self-reliance; and a focus on inexpensive and rapidly realised projects (Chin and Frolic, 2007, 4). Exceptionally, China also financed and supported some major infrastructural projects in Africa, including, in 1967, the 2,000-kilometre Tanzania-Zambia Railway, which, at $406 million, was the PRC's largest foreign aid project at the time (Yu, 1988, 854).

The PRC's Africa policy was significantly diminished during the Great Proletarian Cultural Revolution (1966–1976). Most ambassadors were returned to Peking in 1966 as the PRC subordinated foreign to domestic policy (Ismael, 1971, 522). Such a shift, allied to ". . . China's inability to provide substantial aid to her friends in Africa weakened her position there considerably" (ibid., 523). As the PRC's influence waned, so that of Taiwan (ROC) grew: in mid-1965, 18 African states had diplomatic relations with Peking, and only 15 with Formosa (Taiwan); by 1967 this had changed to 15 and 19, respectively, as ROC aid superseded that of the PRC (ibid., 524).

Sino-African political and economic relations were rekindled after 1967, with a greater emphasis placed on economic co-operation than ideological principles (Jiang, 2014; Dreher and Fuchs, 2015), even though one of the key motivations for the refocus on Africa was the deterioration in relations with the Soviet Union in the late 1960s and the use of Africa as a "battleground in the Sino-Soviet struggle" (Yu, 1988, 851) as part of the internationalisation of its anti-Soviet policy (ibid., 854) which included seeking to build the Third World as a united front against the superpowers (ibid., 855). Development assistance once again became the key instrument of China's Africa policy, but with a stronger alignment with China's own national interests (Chin and Frolic, 2007, 4) including a more overt *quid pro quo* of aid in exchange for supporting the PRC's aspiration to become a member state of the United Nations (Yu, 1988, 852). In November 1971 the People's Republic of China replaced the Republic of China as the representative of China at the United Nations following UN General Assembly Resolution 2758, in part due to the support given by African states: of the 76 votes to replace the ROC by the PRC on the UN Security Council, 26 were contributed by African members of the United Nations. Chairman Mao is reputed to have exclaimed: "it is our African brothers that carried us into the UN!" (Hanauer and Morris, 2014, 7). By the end of 1975, 37 out of 48 African states had formally recognised the PRC as the legitimate representative of China (Yu, 1988, 855).

The Transitional Era (Mid-1970s to the 1990s)

The end of the Cultural Revolution and the death of Mao Zedong in 1976 ushered in a period of uncertainty and introspection in the PRC which was reflected in foreign policy, and which initially dampened the fervour of Sino-African relations (Muekalia, 2004, 7). Within a couple of years the new leader, Deng Xiaoping, had presented a programme of sweeping domestic reforms to the Eleventh Party Congress of the Communist Party (December 1978), the implementation of which, and the domestic economic problems they were intended to confront, would see the financial resources for foreign assistance diverted to internal economic restructuring for the best part of two decades (Davies *et al.*, 2008, 3). Deng emphasised that large-scale assistance to Africa could be the task for China's next generation once China had succeeded with her own development (Jiang, 2014, 58). With the ending of the Cold War, Africa had also lost its strategic value as a bolster for support against the Soviet Union (Taylor, 1998).

As China embarked on its associated 'Open Doors' strategy, the principles underpinning foreign relations shifted from ideological and representational considerations towards the pursuit of mutual economic benefit (Dreher and Fuchs, 2015, 9) emanating from a shifting world order where China sought to counter the ascendancy of the USA by building a multipolar world (Muekalia, 2004, 7). Deng Xiaoping held a much more open attitude towards the West, and was eager to normalise economic and trade relations in order to integrate into the existing international political and economic system dominated by Western capitalism (Chen, 2013, 36). Whilst the underlying principle of China's international economic relations became 'influence without interference' (Qian and Wu, 2007, 1), the country's relations with the continent of Africa shifted significantly to the pursuit of economic opportunities for Chinese firms which could also help kickstart Africa's recovery from its 'lost decade' of debt-induced stagnation and the angst of Structural Adjustment Programmes (Abiru, 2018). According to David Haroz (2011, 69), "China [wanted] Africa to develop, not only for Africa's benefit, but also because a modernized Africa [could] be good for China".

To this end, the 1980s and 1990s saw an intensification of official visits from China to Africa, and from Africa to China (Muekalia, 2004, 7–8; Haroz, 2011, 67), commencing with then Premier Zhao Ziyang's visit to 11 African nations in 1982, during which the mantra of mutually beneficial partnerships was frequently expressed (Yu, 1988; Jiang, 2014). In the process, China's involvement in Africa broadened from development assistance to joint commercial ventures, political and military co-operation, trade and investment, technology transfer and training, as well as cultural exchange (Haroz, 2011, 65–67). Reform of state-owned enterprises (SOEs) in China from the early 1990s created fresh financial imperatives; their expansion into overseas markets provided a much-needed means of generating revenue (Haroz, 2011, 69). A particular emphasis was given to Africa's resource-producing nations and the wealthier states which represented promising consumer markets for Chinese products (Muekalia, 2004, 7). Preferential loans to African governments became conditional on China being granted access to Africa-based enterprises (ibid., 8). China's participation in the Africa Development Bank, which it joined in 1985, provided an additional conduit for involvement in development and infrastructure projects across the continent. Meanwhile, China's financial sector reforms in 1994 created three new state-controlled banks[5] which provided the financial means for China's growing internationalisation strategy (Haroz, 2011, 69).

The Sino-Africa New Age (the Twenty-First Century)

Three key developments have come to define China-Africa relations in the Twenty-First Century. The formalisation of China's 'Go-Out' (or Go Global) policy in 1999 gave 'China Inc.' (both private and state-owned enterprises) the green light to seek investment opportunities in African markets (Seyfried, 2019; Grimm, 2014). Chinese outward foreign direct investment (COFDI) in Africa has increased steadily since the beginning of the present century: for instance, flows increased from $317 million in 2004 (5.7% of total COFDI) to $5,490 million in 2008 (9.8%), whilst the total stock of COFDI in China grew from $899 million in 2004 to $13,042 million in 2010,[6] and reached $44,000 million in 2019 (UNCTAD, 2021).

The creation of the Forum on China – Africa Cooperation (FOCAC) in 2000 has strongly reaffirmed China's commitment to the African continent, and has institutionalised bilateral connections between China and African states under a more formal framework, at the same time cementing China's

Go-Out strategy to encourage and support Chinese firms venturing over-seas. Although FOCAC clearly supports China's globalisation efforts, the idea of creating a 'one-to-multiple' mechanism to oversee relations between China and Africa was originally suggested by African leaders and diplo-mats (Li, 2012b). Initially the Chinese government was reluctant to adopt the idea, as multilateral cooperation would be difficult to coordinate, but the economic and strategic value of strengthened Sino-African relations set against China's need to secure sources of raw materials and expand markets for its products convinced the leadership of the FOCAC's potential value as a counterbalance to established Africa-focused institutional mechanisms such as the Franco-African Summit, the Tokyo International Conference on African Development, the Commonwealth Conference, the European-African Summit and the US African Growth and Opportunity Act (Bodomo, 2019).

A FOCAC Summit takes place every three years, which functions as a platform to announce new initiatives and strategies between China and Africa to be implemented over the ensuing three-year period. The most recent FOCAC VII in Beijing in 2018, on the theme 'China and Africa: Toward an Even Stronger Community with a Shared Future through Win-Win Cooperation' saw President Xi Jinping outline his 'Eight Major Initiatives' for future collaboration with Africa: industrial promotion; infra-structure connectivity; trade facilitation; green development; capacity building; healthcare; people-to-people exchange; and peace and security (Ministry of Foreign Affairs, PRC, 2018). The summit was also the first time in decades that almost all (53 out of 54, with Swaziland the only absen-tee) African country leaders had gathered in Beijing (Seyfried, 2019). At the time of writing, there is an assumption that the eighth FOCAC Summit will be held online due to the COVID-19 pandemic, and it is likely that post-pandemic recovery efforts will be a priority focus (FOCAC, 2020).

The activities of FOCAC incorporate the third key development, the Belt and Road Initiative (BRI), emanating from China that has implications for Africa. Introduced in 2013, the BRI originally centred on the historic terrestrial and maritime Silk Roads which connected China with Asia, the Middle East, Europe and, as we saw in Section 1.1, Africa. The BRI quickly evolved into a global mechanism for improving infrastructure in develop-ing countries using finance provided by two of China's policy banks (the China Development Bank and the Export-Import Bank of China) and pri-vate sector actors supporting the PRC's Going Global strategy. Following the theme of the seventh FOCOC summit in 2018, the BRI is presented as a win-win cooperation strategy: infrastructure deficiencies are a major con-straint on development in Africa, whilst in helping to ease such constraints by building roads, railways, hydropower schemes and so on, China is able to mobilise excess domestic savings and provide an external outlet for its underemployed construction and heavy industry sectors, whilst at the same time opening up new avenues for trade as Africa develops, and winning friends and gaining influence on the African continent (Dollar, 2019, 2). In 2016, one-third of total external finance for infrastructure construction in Africa was provided by China, and more than 10,000 Chinese-owned firms are currently operating across the continent (ibid., 3).

The involvement of Africa in the BRI has not been without criticism, however. Borrowing from China for large-scale infrastructure projects has significantly increased the debt burden of several African countries, raising the spectre of what has been called 'debt-trap diplomacy' (Taylor and Zajontz, 2020, 277). China's funding of development infrastructure in Africa lacks the transparency that is typically required in international development assistance (Githaiga *et al.*, 2019), and in 2014 there were almost 100,000 Chinese workers engaged in the various China-funded infrastructure projects across a continent where local unemployment levels are often quite high (Dollar, 2019, 3). The view from China is quite different, however: "China-Africa relations are characterised by summit diplomacy, equality, co-development and institutionalisation of cooperation" (Li, 2019, 52).

1.3 China and South African Political and Economic Relations: An Institutional Transition View

Introduction: South Africa and China's Comparative Transitions

This section will set the scene for the empirical case studies that follow. It will present an introductory and comparative discussion of the transition process in South Africa and China, with a particular focus on institutions. The narrative will place the actions of South African business firms in historical context, taking us through the colonial, Apartheid and post-Apartheid eras, showing how the changing political environment created the conditions and institutional arrangements that helped to shape the country's business sector, both domestically and internationally. Along the same timeline, we will also present some of the background to China's own economic transition, looking in particular at some of the implications of the shifts in China's political economy for the array of institutions, both formal and informal, which play a key role in the process of economic development.

There are clear connections between the domestic process of transition, or political-economic evolution, and the character of the two nations' engagement with international markets. Economic sanctions during the Apartheid era severely constrained where and how much South Africa could participate in the emerging new international division of labour which was already well advanced by the time sanctions ended in 1993. Meanwhile, South Africa's position as an important ally of the West during the Cold War, together with its recognition of Taiwan until 1998, significantly constrained the scope of South Africa's engagement with China's emerging market, which itself was the product of a thoroughgoing process of internal reform and transition.

Table 1.1 summarises the key phases of political and economic transition that have taken place in South Africa and China since the beginning of the Twentieth Century. One of the key observations to draw from this summary is that, although both countries have been through some quite profound changes in both the political and economic spheres, the only real point of convergence between the two processes of transition has occurred when both countries started to become more fully integrated into the global economic system (leaving aside their respective, but largely unconnected phases of internationalisation during the imperialist era). It is true that there was some common ground between the two countries before the turn of the century: for instance, the South African Communist Party maintained contact with the Chinese Communist Party even during the Apartheid era (Ellis, 2013, 2). But in general both the regression (by mainstream international standards) and the reform processes that both countries have been through have occurred in parallel rather than in tandem. But there are common elements. Both countries have sought to rid themselves of the shackles of foreign dominance, although in quite different contexts and in starkly different ways. Both have gone through a period of international isolation, and both have had to draw themselves back from the extremes of Apartheid and Totalitarianism, respectively, in order to appear more acceptable to a global economic system which, during the neoliberal era in particular, set very clear political-economic standards to which participants were expected to adhere. Both are relative late-comers to the globalised international market, which has required both to be particularly nimble in the way they negotiate the hurdles of a highly competitive global economic system. South Africa has relied on the quality and desirability of its resources, goods, services and skills array as it has sought to penetrate the lucrative Chinese market; meanwhile China has invested huge sums in the African continent to pave its own way towards urgently needed natural resources and new consumer markets. The coalescence of the two countries' respective journeys through transition and reform, to the point where they now constitute two important pillars of the BRICS (Brazil, Russia, India and China) emerging economies, has increasingly been cemented by the high-level bilateral conversations between South Africa and China, such as the South Africa – China Bi-National Commission, which was inaugurated in 2001.

Table 1.1 South Africa and China's Comparative Transitions

Timeline From 1900	South African Political-Economic Transitions	Implications for South African Business	Chinese Political-Economic Transitions	Implications for Business in China
Before 1950	Late British colonial era; extractive industry boom	Early business environments regulated by the British-built institutional system, esp. the 'rule of law'. The mining sector became the primary economic growth engine.	CCP became the ruling party	Central government economic planning to recover from war and civil strife. All business owned and controlled by the State under the command economy. Economic inefficiency, structural inertia.
1950s to Late 1970s	Apartheid era (boom period)	Manufacturing developed fast under State support and protection. Family conglomerates and institutional groups in mining, retailing and financial industries began to play an important role in shaping the business and even political institutional environments of South Africa.	Cultural Revolution & isolationism	Promulgation of communist ideology across the country. Close connections with other communist countries brought extra burden to China's economic development. The 'Great Leap Forward' in the 1950s as well as the Cultural Revolution between 1966 and 1976 caused widespread economic stagnation and structural regression.
1980 to 1993	Apartheid era (international sanctions)	Mining less central to economic growth. Declining outputs & performance of public corporations. Rand appreciation widened the deficit in international trade. Sanctions isolated S. Africa from international markets. Overseas capital flight via large conglomerates.	Open Door policy	First trial of economic reform in the eastern coastal area with the creation of 'Special Economic Zones' where preferential incentive policies were introduced to encourage inward FDI and joint ventures with foreign firms. Tentative commencement of SOE reform.

(*Continued*)

Table 1.1 (Continued)

Timeline From 1900	South African Political-Economic Transitions	Implications for South African Business	Chinese Political-Economic Transitions	Implications for Business in China
1994 to 2001	Post-Apartheid era (restructuring, redistribution, reconciliation)	A number of macro-level policies (RDP, GEAR, BEE) introduced by ANC. Partially achieved the aim of rebalancing political power, but many economic objectives have failed to materialise through lack of institutional capacity at all levels, hindering business efficiency.	Consolidation of economic reforms	Spread of the reform process to other coastal provinces. Gradual liberalisation of the 'socialist market economy', rapid private sector growth. Reform of institutional environment, in part to prepare for WTO accession. Rapid economic growth.
2001 to 2010	Re-connection to the world economy	Rising new middle class, including black business elites, exacerbates internal inequality. Increase in bilateral and multilateral agreements with international institutions (e.g. BRICS). High-level South Africa-China economic dialogue encourages business cooperation.	WTO accession and further engagement with Africa through FOCAC	Strengthening of formal institutions and gradual weakening of state-imposed constraints on foreign investment, trade and industrial production. Massive investment in infrastructure. Continued rapid economic growth. Investment incentive policies treat foreign & domestic firms equally.
2011 to Present	Economic stagnation and rebounding process	Internal political turmoil and persistent government debts hindered economic development, and large SEOs in key sectors struggled to grow. New President Cyril Ramaphosa vowed to concentrate on recovering the economy by tackling corruption and fighting against socioeconomic inequality.	Ascending economic power in Africa and overall BRI strategies	China's overall vision towards Africa is strategised through the infrastructure-centred BRI. The extent of collaboration with Africa is beyond trade and investment but also on humanitarian projects such as health, education and social exchange.

Constriction to Autonomy (1866 to 1948)

South Africa: Late British Colonial Era and the Mineral Revolution

Following the discovery of precious mineral resources, primarily diamonds and gold, in the mid/late Nineteenth Century, South Africa became one of the richest resource-endowed countries in the world, and for many decades the South African economy was, and to a degree remains, highly structured around its natural resource advantages. The country's resource richness was an important magnet to financial investment from and ultimately political control by external parties, and it was these that had a profound influence on the shaping and definition of South Africa's emerging institutional environment from the mid-Nineteenth Century onwards. In this sense, there has been a two-way interaction between the business and institutional environments: influential business actors and organisations (conglomerates) have historically dovetailed almost seamlessly with governance practices and agendas, creating an institutional landscape which fundamentally served their best interests; meanwhile, these institutions and, within them, institutional practices have in turn defined the character and, most particularly, the political and ethnic orientation of the business sector. The following paragraphs will illuminate this interrelationship of business and institutions by looking at South Africa's late colonial history and the so-called 'mineral revolution', which helps provide context to how the changing institutional environment across time has influenced the present business environment in South Africa.

During the war-torn years of the late Nineteenth Century, conflicts between different populations and races intensified due to competition for natural resources and territory (Worden, 2012). The country became anchored by the increasing inflows of international capital into the mining sector as well as associated financial industries, with the British the most proactive European pursuer of South Africa's gold resources. Upon seizing political control, the British colonial government introduced new institutional systems to South Africa to facilitate trade and industrial production, for example trades unions as well as various customs and tariff arrangements. In the meantime, South Africa had also entered a period of industrialisation which was initiated by the government in order to promote a manufacturing sector for the purpose of strengthening the country's self-sufficiency through nurturing its own industrial base (Hamilton *et al.*, 2010).

However, the many stimulus initiatives and protectionist policies made by the government towards the secondary (especially manufacturing) sector in South Africa were not very effective, and contributed little to the country's GDP, largely because the secondary industrial sector was built on weak foundations (Hamilton *et al.*, 2010): a small domestic market size and a shortage of skilled/semi-skilled workers due to limitations in the quality and extent of education and professional training. A colour bar became one of the main features of the political agenda of the British colonial government, which created an institutional environment that favoured the White population and protected their jobs, land and other resources under their control (Worden, 2012). We will see later in this book that there are still some circumstances where privileged access to important and influential political actors continues to bestow advantages to some business actors in their dealings with the Chinese market (e.g. Case A, Chapter 3).

Based on a coalition between the National Party and the Labour Party, the Pact government that came to power in 1924 tried to foster secondary industry by using different incentives. The government started to intervene into the industrial sector, and heralded the birth of many large state-owned companies: for example the Electricity Supply Commission (ESCOM) and the Iron and Steel Industrial Corporation (ISCOR) (Worden, 2012). These companies subsequently came to dominate and control the country's rail networks, infrastructural construction, gas and electricity utilities and so on. They also started producing the fundamental materials needed to enable South Africa to evolve into a more sophisticated industrialisation stage. This resulted in a growth in output which started to peak just before the Great Depression of 1929 (Fine and Rustomjee, 1996). The Great Depression drastically affected the South African economy, particularly in the first 15 months (1929–1930), but gold cushioned South Africa to a certain extent, and this enabled her economy to recover from the recession more quickly than many other nations (Feinstein, 2005, 121–122). South Africa was also one of the few countries in the world that materially were only affected by the Second World War to a limited extent.

Apart from the political changes which have contributed to institutional transitions in South African economic history, the mineral revolution (which dated from the second half of the Nineteenth Century) also contributed to the formation of new institutional systems and mechanisms in the Republic. Many of the institutional foundations built during that time still have a considerable impact on social development in South Africa today, and this is typically manifested in the business sector. To a certain extent, even today, the South African institutional framework is still associated with British institutions mainly because of the early British settlers' institutional legacies. However, even though the institutional framework was built to serve and enhance economic development, the institutional mechanism was not immune from the general social grime: racial discrimination was the 'snake' coiled into all institutions established in South Africa during this period, and this feature, which continued to manifest itself for almost half a century, was deeply rooted into the government's policies during the ascendancy of the National Party (NP) with the introduction and implementation of the Apartheid regime in South Africa.

China: Journey From an Empire to a Republic

On a parallel timescale, China and South Africa had little direct intersection apart from their common experience of British colonial influence. In the present context, 1840 might be seen as a turning point in Chinese late imperial history. The Anglo-Chinese War (First Opium War), as a catalyst, accelerated changes to the Chinese political and economic landscape over the ensuing 100 years. From the decline of the late Qing Empire to the turbulence of the warlord period, from the Anti-Japanese War to the Civil War between the Kuomintang and the Communist Party, Chinese society was in a constant state of institutional flux until the establishment of the Communist Party of China (CPC). The political strategy led by Mao Zedong focusing on peasant farmers as a revolutionary force in a then-predominantly agrarian society eventually became key to the ascendancy of the CPC as the ruling party in China. The CPC is well versed in the principle of 'who wins the hearts of the people, wins the world'.

Self-Reliance and International Re-Connection (1948 to 1994)

South Africa – Apartheid Regime

Following their victory in the 1948 elections, the National Party (NP) charted South Africa's development path for more than four decades. The Apartheid regime, perhaps one of the most controversial political policies the world has seen, was a system of racial segregation dividing the country's ethnic groups, which was implemented by the NP and its successors, formalising the colour bar by means of a set of institutional regulations. Apartheid became the symbolic feature of South African society until 1994 when the first free national elections were held.

In the early Apartheid era, the South African economy saw an unprecedented acceleration, especially during the post-war years (Wolpe, 1972), and reached a peak in the early 1970s. Aided by state support, protection and preferential policies, the manufacturing sectors developed rapidly during the early Apartheid period (Feinstein, 2005, 172–173), which contrasted sharply with the situation in the world economy as a whole which stagnated somewhat during the height of the Cold War. In South Africa, several parastatal (state-owned and state-controlled) enterprises were established to operate in conjunction with those that had been set up in the early Twentieth

Century, among the first of which were the Electricity Supply Commission (Eskom) and the South African Iron and Steel Corporation (Iscor), which were both established in the 1920s, and the Industrial Development Corporation (IDC), which was an institution founded in 1940 to facilitate new start-ups in the industrial sector (Fine and Rustomjee, 1996). Through the IDC's business assistance function, many other state companies were established such as the South African Coal, Oil and Gas Corporation (SASOL), the Southern Oil Exploration Corporation (Soekor), the Phosphate Development Corporation (Foskor), and so on (ibid.). During this time, particularly from the early 1950s until the mid-1970s, the state government thus actively intervened in many large home-grown companies that were created, fostered and developed with generous support for the purpose of making the manufacturing sector the new catalyst for the country's economy to enable it to achieve self-reliance.

Along with these parastatal enterprises, this period also saw the expansion of Afrikaaner capitalism as well as the development of the financial sector. Many family conglomerates and institutional groups in mining, retail and the financial industries, in addition to contributing to the country's economic growth, also played an important role in shaping the business and even the political institutional environments of South Africa at the time (Makgetla and Seidman, 1980). Between them, these major business enterprises accumulatively accounted for approximately 80 per cent of the total value of the Johannesburg Stock Exchange (JSE) (Hanlon, 1986, 67), of which Sanlam and Rembrandt were representative of Afrikaner capital whilst the others were originally built upon British investment. Quite clearly, therefore, a small number of very large and monopolistic family-based conglomerates came to dominate the South African business landscape during the Apartheid era. This illustrates the institutional legacy of the Apartheid era, and in particular highlights the very close connections that developed between business and the state which, as we will see in Chapter 3, helped to strengthen South Africa's institutional landscape but at a cost to wider concerns about social and distributive justice.

After this period of business expansion and consolidation up to the 1970s, the economy began to struggle, entering a period of stagnation for more than 10 years from 1980. In 1994, when most developed countries had more or less completed their recovery from the privations of the Cold War, South Africa's economic performance reached rock bottom, being by this time worse than the situation in 1981 (Fine and Rustomjee, 1996). The Apartheid regime caused the county to lose international support from its historical political and economic partners. South Africa's international isolation contributed to a period when economic self-reliance became increasingly important, and this was further reflected in the country's evolving institutional matrix.

China: From Planned Economy to Open-Door Policy
(1949–1994)

On the other side of the globe, China underwent a thoroughgoing process of transition which more or less ran parallel to the timeline just described for South Africa. However, that is where any similarities largely end. After the CPC became the ruling party, China went into a period of 'forced self-reliance' partly due to the communist ideology which was opposed by most western nations. China also experienced a series of internal political revolutions, which caused some turbulent social disorder and hence economic stagnation. The key episode in the transition process commences with the reforms initiated by Deng Xiaoping in 1978. Deng's reforms were stimulated, arguably necessitated, by growing problems of economic stagnation, unemployment and income inequality, and commenced with an incremental and subsequently thoroughgoing overhaul of the agrarian sector (Story, 2004, 127), with market-based financial incentives used to counter and rectify the stifling impact of the command economy on growth, diversification and innovation. Market rationality also gradually, but only patchily and often quite half-heartedly, became applied to the SOE (state-owned enterprise) sector. Whilst the state, under the guise of the CPC, pushed with increasing fervour the opening-up of the national economy after 1993, simultaneous pressure for and movement towards political reform was brutally suppressed, not least in Tiananmen Square on 4 June 1989. Democratisation and the development of civil society have hardly progressed in China since then, with the party-state at the apex of a very sharply pointed socio-political pyramid (ibid., 130), whilst the country has nonetheless grown to be one of the largest and fastest-growing economies in the world. SOE reform became a policy priority in 1997, in part because of widespread corruption, and partly in anticipation of China's accession to the World Trade Organization in 2001, which obliged further reforms in the financial sector and opened up market access to foreign goods.

One of the key differences between the China and South Africa during this reform period lies in the extent to which economic transformation in China has proceeded apace, but (unlike in South Africa during the post-Apartheid period, as we shall see) without any parallel substantive reform of the political system: the CPC has proven to be remarkably durable throughout the process of transformation (Naughton, 2008, 91). Barry Naughton (2008) in fact argues that, far from being a passive bystander as the economic transition took on its own shape, logic and momentum, the CPC actually shaped the economic reform process is such a way as to underpin, rather than undermine, the position and power of key political actors within the system. Political patronage became the key means of achieving this end, whereby newly influential economic actors became tied to the existing regime and system, in exchange for financial reward and smooth progress through political and bureaucratic minefields laid by the regime itself (ibid., 91). Whilst this agenda may have helped to hold the Chinese political economy together, there have been significant costs and compromises which have over time come to serve as significant impediments to the smooth and efficient running of the economy, and which foreign firms in particular have often found it difficult to negotiate.

Foreign companies entering the Chinese markets have to run the gauntlet of an economy which is tightly controlled by the party-state, which regulates markets and has a controlling interest in the financial system (banks, insurance and securities) (Story, 2004, 132), as well as strategic policy direction and the arbitration of conflicts and disputes. The monopoly position that the CPC has maintained since 1949, and the way that the Party has frequently used its power to underpin its own strategic and institutional interests, has resulted in very low levels of trust being shown by private businesses and public citizens towards officials and the institutional organs of the state (ibid.). Thus, the picture that emerges is one of a rapid transition of China's economy from central planning to market liberalism, paralleled by a rigid perpetuation of the political regime with little more than lip service being paid to the need for political reform. Inasmuch as the political system maps out the shape, form and function of the formal institutions which facilitate and regulate economic activity, this political inertia has significant consequences for, in the present context, companies entering the Chinese markets from the international arena: "managers in foreign corporations cannot take institutions for granted" (Story, 2004, 136). The government retains for itself considerable scope for making decisions, granting privileges, taking actions and enforcing restrictions which suit its own interests, or its self-portrait picture of the strategic 'national interest', and this has, *inter alia*, created an environment within which corruption and nepotism have become rife among public officials. As we shall see a little later in this chapter, this simultaneously creates an atmosphere of uncertainty and insecurity for foreign businesses, large and small, whilst at the same time encouraging or obliging the deployment of informal institutional practices in order to smooth the operation of the socialist market economy. Domestic firms, especially those operating in the private sector, face similar hurdles and impediments, but in general are more inured to operating in the prevailing environment and, through experience and a more intimate familiarity with the prevailing socio-cultural situation, seem to possess the requisite knowledge and contact networks to enable them to function and survive, aided, of course, by a hitherto buoyant economy.

Globalisation and South-South Cooperation (1994 to Present)

South Africa: The Post-Apartheid Era

The victory of the ANC in 1994 and the successful election of Nelson Mandela as South African president turned South African history to a new page. It was a gargantuan task for the new government to restore the 'broken' country to order. Nonetheless, almost 30 years since the accession of the ANC, many questions remain over its record of achievement in re-establishing the country's social, political and economic status. The ANC has indeed done an excellent job of dealing with the social problems of racial segmentation by dismantling the colour bar that had haunted the majority black South Africans for centuries. The formerly exiled ANC party gained political popularity and support through its proposal to establish a democratic country for all South African people, creating a new country "that is unified, open, non-racial, non-sexist, democratic and free", and with a Constitution that should meet the principles of "equality, mutual respect, dignity and promotion of basic human rights" (African National Congress official website).

In terms of foreign policy, the ANC realised the new world order required new permutations in their political stance, especially after centuries of international sanction and isolation during the Apartheid era. The end of the Cold War disconnected the ANC from their historical international communist allies, and the emergence of the new Triad economic blocs (North America, the European Union and Japan-led East Asia) provided the ANC with new challenges within the global political order: to follow the principle of being non-aligned, nor associated with any international military blocs, but meanwhile actively pursuing international economic cooperation; transforming South Africa from its Apartheid era isolation into full membership of the international community; performing the role of regional leader in a peaceful and cooperative manner, and fostering multilateral economic relationships with other African countries within the region.

The economic dimension, which provides the institutional backdrop against which South African outward investment should be viewed, the general economic policy of the ANC has been to pursue a growth and development path in order to create a robust, balanced and dynamic economic environment within which poverty and inequality could be eliminated, through two fundamental strategies: redistribution of resources to improve living standards for the majority South African population; and restructuring the South African economy in both the public and private sectors. This also became the guiding principle for other ANC economic policies, especially those affecting the domestic economy. Internationally, the ANC proposed to adopt an 'open' policy in order to rebuild foreign investors' confidence towards South Africa, granting foreign investors the same level of facilitation that domestic firms enjoyed. One notion that emerged from the ANC's new economic policies that reflected an important feature of an economy undergoing institutional transition was 'flexibility', as stated in the ANC policy guidelines as it prepared for government in the mid-1990s:

> In the context of the growth and development strategy, the role of the state should be adjusted to the needs of the national economy in a flexible way. The primary question in this regard is not the legal form that state involvement in economic activity might take at any point, but whether such actions will strengthen the ability of the economy to respond to the massive inequalities in the country, relieve the material hardship of the majority of the people, and stimulate economic growth and competitiveness.
>
> (ANC, 1992)

The results from the latest election in 2019, in which the ANC gained just 57.5% of the vote, its worst ever result, suggest that its performance in these regards has been disappointing when set against the very laudable objectives. Table 1.2 summarises some key institutional themes relevant to the business sector and looks selectively at certain of the ANC's economic policies that have been introduced to South Africa over the last 30 years.

Along with a quite significant shift in the balance of political power in post-Apartheid South Africa, there have been several hitherto largely unsuccessful attempts to bring about restructuring and redistribution, principally along racial lines. Many of the underlying economic objectives have failed to materialise to the extent originally envisioned by the country's new political leaders. There is also both an institutional background and a set of institutional consequences to this. However, the formal institutional environment in South Africa has regressed more or less across the board from the quite high standards that were a feature of the country before and during the Apartheid era, especially within the financial market (Schwab, 2019). Whilst some SOEs suffered mismanagement under Zuma's presidency, they continue to follow monopolistic business practices, and the business sector retains a powerful influence on political policy-making processes.

China: Open Doors and Unprecedented Development

Four decades or so on from the reforms initiated by Deng Xiaoping, China is hardly recognisable from the economic behemoth it was at the end of the Cultural Revolution in 1976. The Fourteenth Party Congress in 1992 formally and firmly pushed towards what became known as the 'socialist

Table 1.2 Key South African Institutional Initiatives in the last 30 Years

Policy and Initiative	Year	Initiated by	Aim	Performance and Progress
Reconstruction and Development Programme	1994	Nelson Mandela (President)	To address the socio-economic issues the country was facing, and to integrate growth, development, reconstruction, redistribution and reconciliation under a unified macroeconomic framework (Corder, 1997).	Has largely failed to meet the majority of South Africans' expectations, due to the lack of capacity in institutions at all levels to implement and manage such a programme, not helped by insufficient funding and inefficient measures for spending these funds (Cameron, 1996).
Growth, Employment and Redistribution	1996	Trevor Manuel (Minister of Finance)	A more neo-liberal approach to fiscal and monetary policy which mainly involved government deficit reduction, exchange rate control and trade (Government of South Africa, 1996).	Disappointing outcomes as policy failed to integrate the key objectives of redistribution, growth and employment with other government strategies (e.g. monetary policy), and thus neglected to appreciate that the impacts of one national issue would act as a constraint on the others (Adelzadeh, 1996).
Affirmative Action	1998	SA Government	To achieve equality in the workplace by eliminating the discrimination against black and coloured people which had caused gross unfairness in employment during the Apartheid regime	Produced another layer of imbalance within the nation among the black people, because the policy has fundamentally benefited only a small segment of the black population, mainly in the small rising black middle class (Alexander, 2007)
Black Economic Empowerment	1998	SA Government	To enhance the nation's socio-economic development (Ponte *et al.*, 2006), with a focus primarily on promoting black ownership and management control in the business sectors, and creating more job opportunities, eliminating poverty and minimising the imbalance of power, wealth and resources between black and white people.	Government was unable to look after the majority mass of the population who stood on the bottom rung of the ladder, but instead simply created small numbers of black business entrepreneur elites, which only worsened the imbalanced conditions not only between the white and black people, but also within the black population itself (Herbst, 2005).

(Continued)

Table 1.2 (Continued)

Policy and Initiative	Year	Initiated by	Aim	Performance and Progress
Accelerated and Shared Growth Initiative for South Africa	2005	Thabo Mbeki (President)	To introduce policies, programmes and interventions that would allow the South African economy to grow enough to halve poverty and unemployment between 2004 and 2014 (Mosala *et al.*, 2017)	Some reasonable success at partial levels but could not sustain these gains due to lack of strategic leadership needed for full implementation.
Broad-Based Black Economic Empowerment	2010	Jacob Zuma (President)	Admitting the failure of BEE policy implementation as a tool to redress the imbalance of power and resource between the 'two nations in South Africa', broader-based policy has been added to form the new BB-BEE, with the hope of making the black empowerment policy more effective across the board in black South Africa.	Main criticism is that the policy tended to benefit those well-connected and wealthy minority, and these 'elites' tended to shut the door to other black people once they had reached their positions of privilege (Bopela, 2009).
New Growth Path	2010	Jacob Zuma (President)	To accelerate growth in the South African economy, with ways rapidly to reduce poverty, unemployment and inequality.	Failed to break the long-standing minerals-energy complex and other key determining features of the post-apartheid economic landscape (e.g. capital flight), so little more than a general policy documented on paper for open debate (Fine, 2012).
National Development Plan – 2030	2013	SA Government	Adopted as the blueprint for a future economic and social development strategy for South Africa, for eliminating poverty and reducing inequality by 2030.	

market economy', which Gary Sigley (2006, 489) has described as being based upon "a hybrid socialist-neoliberal . . . form of political rationality that is at once authoritarian . . . yet, at the same time, seeks to govern certain subjects, but not all, through their own autonomy." It is during this phase that China's institutional environment started to evolve in order to try to catch up with the reformists' political-economic ideals. This 'catching-up' process of institutional evolution continued into the next phase of China's economic reforms, which commenced with the country's accession to the World Trade Organization in 2001, after which China had (as much as it was able and willing) increasingly to measure itself against and comply with international institutional standards and practices. As the reform process has unfolded, therefore, foreign companies that have been drawn to the Chinese market have had to negotiate an ever-changing landscape of institutional structures and procedures.

To summarise, this chapter provides a general contextual background to the book. It commences with a short historical account of Sino-African historical connections, before bringing Sino-African political relations into the discussion. The subsequent discussion of internal political and economic conditions and the way they have influenced bilateral relationships provides an important historical backdrop to the more recent phase when South African businesses have started to venture further and deeper into the international market, albeit only reaching China to any significant extent since the early 2000s. The complex and occasionally uneasy interface of politics (and political agendas) and economics (and thus the business setting) between the two nations helps to explain how and why institutions have rather inconsistently served to support and facilitate both domestic and international business activities. The respective transitions of these two countries from an institutional perspective, looked at individually and comparatively, identifies key elements which help build a framework for the empirical case studies in Chapter Three.

Notes

1. The seven voyages were undertaken between 1405 and 1433. The first of these to reach Africa, specifically the coasts of present-day Somalia and Kenya, took place between 1417 and 1419.
2. A conflict in the Talas Valley of Kyrgyzstan between the forces of the Abbasid Caliphate and the Tibetan Empire against those of the Tang Chinese as the latter sought, unsuccessfully, to expand westwards into Central Asia.
3. A loose group of economically deprived Asian, African and South American nations that were not aligned with American capitalism or Soviet socialism.
4. The Republic of China (ROC) was a charter member of the United Nations in 1945, and continued to represent China on the international body after the civil

war and the formation of the People's Republic in 1949. Both adopted a 'One China' stance, which stymied the possibility of dual representation, and so with significant support from the United States the ROC remained the sole representative of China at the UN until being replaced by the PRC in 1971.

5. The China Development Bank, the China Export Import Bank and the China Agricultural Development Bank.

6. China, Ministry of Commerce, 2011, *2010 Statistical Bulletin of China's Outward Foreign Direct Investment*.

2 Institutional Environments and an Institutional Model

Sino-African relations have received growing academic attention across various disciplines over the last three to four decades. Scholars in the field of International Relations (IR) have engaged issues ranging from resource extraction to military security, foreign assistance, bilateral trade and foreign investment (Raposo *et al.*, 2018; Manji and Marks, 2007; Rotberg, 2008; Shinn and Eisenman, 2012; Alden and Large, 2019; Jenkins, 2019; Carmody, 2016; Oqubay and Lin, 2019; Adem, 2014; Ampiah and Naidu, 2008; Raine, 2009). Such research has tended to be focused at the level of the nation-state and inter-state relations, whereas discussions from a business perspective have been rather less prominent. Some specialists in International Business (IB) studies are starting to show and interest in the emerging country markets and the so-called third wave of international business interactions (Jansson, 2007, 1) where multinational enterprises from mature markets shift their focus towards the emerging markets (e.g. China, Russia, India, South Africa), whilst firms from emerging country markets are also expanding their international business operations. Within the Sino-African context, most research interest has concentrated on China's business engagement with Africa (Abegunrin and Manyeruke, 2020; Rotberg, 2008; Xiang, 2018; Yu, 1977; Abdulai, 2017; Carmody *et al.*, 2020; Oqubay and Lin, 2019; Lee, 2017; April and Shelton, 2014; Tang, 2020; Alden, 2007; Xabadiya and Hu, 2019; Sandry and Edinger, 2009), with much less emphasis placed on individual African countries' business relations with China. The present study aims to make a contribution to filling this latter research lacuna. A particular emphasis will be placed on the role that institutions, both formal and informal, play in international business activities and strategies.

DOI: 10.4324/9781003165668-2

2.1 An Institutional Perspective in International Business Studies

A Brief Introduction

From the outset of my research on South African business involvement in China I sensed the need for an alternative approach to conventional IB frameworks, which place a heavy emphasis on quantitative research methods (Doz, 2011), most particularly because the data on foreign direct investment (FDI) flows required for rigorous statistical analysis were neither accessible nor robust enough to make such an approach viable. Both the South African and Chinese governments place considerable emphasis on volumes of bilateral trade, but much less attention is given to flows and performance of FDI between the two countries. South Africa has only had formal diplomatic relations with the PRC since 1998. South Africa-China business relationships have only gained momentum since 2000 and are only now beginning to assume a relatively significant scale.[1] Obtaining reliable data on these nascent and hitherto limited business ties is a challenge: although some indicative FDI figures are available from each country's statistical bureaux or central banks, these tend to be aggregated, are somewhat inconsistent across time, and often adopt different methodologies of calculation. As a result of these constraints, I chose to adopt a multidisciplinary and largely qualitative research approach which focuses on the role of institutions in South African firms' business involvement with the Chinese markets.

Conventional IB research derives from its historical association with the 'triad economies' (North America, Western Europe and Japan) and their expanding overseas business connections. Early IB research focused on transaction costs and neoclassical economics (Tihanyi *et al.*, 2012, 33). Several classic IB theories and paradigms were developed by IB scholars in the US and Europe to help better understand the foreign investment activities of multi-national corporations (MNCs): Hymer's (1960) Monopolistic Advantage Theory was the first contribution to the study of FDI; the OLI (ownership, location, internalisation) paradigm developed by Dunning (1980, 2000; Dunning and Lundan, 2008a) provided an analytical framework to explain why a multinational enterprise (MNE) would conduct a particular foreign investment activity in a particular location; Buckley and Casson (1976, 2002, 2009) have demonstrated that MNEs tend to maximise their profits by internalising foreign markets in their Internalisation Theory; meanwhile the Uppsala Model is more directed at decision-making, the main idea of this model being the internationalisation of firms through gradual learning (Johanson and Vahlne, 1977, 2009; Welch *et al.*, 2016). These research outcomes all relied on the ability to collect a large volume of timely, consistent and wide-ranging data to allow rigorous quantitative analysis.

Undeniably, classic IB theories can offer general explanations on questions such as the driving forces of MNCs investing abroad in seeking natural resources, markets, efficiency and strategic assets, but these have less validity and value when applied to late movers, such as South African firms engaging with the Chinese market. Such a process cannot simply be distilled to economic and financial variables: a whole raft of contextual social, cultural and political factors, actors and structures also have a significant bearing on decisions and actions when it comes to emerging country markets such as South Africa and China (and, indeed, mature markets as well) (Tihanyi *et al.*, 2012). This underpins my desire to include the contextual, and most particularly the institutional environment in my exploration of South African firms' adventurous journeys to and within China. Institutions both facilitate and hinder business interactions, and certainly cannot be overlooked in transnational business dealings, most particularly in the context of transitional economies where a combination of the old and the new, the insular and the international, provides a contextual landscape that has to be negotiated with skill and dexterity if business ventures are to succeed. China, for instance, has been undergoing a fast-paced transformation to a market-driven economy, yet still remains firmly in the grip of central planning driven, at least in principle, by a socialist ideology (Xu, 2011; Gong and Sullivan, 2017); whilst in the case of South Africa, the policies which underpin its economic transition have significant political and ethnic underpinnings (Mosala *et al.*, 2017). To comprehend South African and Chinese business interactions within two economic contexts with quite complex institutional environments requires a multi-dimensional investigation of "the intersection of policies and business and effectiveness of different government systems" (Tihanyi *et al.*, 2012, 40).

In addition, the prevalence of informality in business dealings within emerging economies was the third reason of introducing an institutional approach to my business investigation. International IB researchers were fairly slow to recognise the importance of informal institutions (such as cultural norms and customs) and other contextual variables in conditioning the overseas business activities of MNCs in emerging economies (Peng and Heath, 1996; Meyer *et al.*, 2009; Doh *et al.*, 2017). A significant volume of recent IB research on Chinese inward FDI highlights the complexity of the Chinese business environment, and acknowledges the need for MNCs to be institutionally sensitive when operating in the Chinese market. Similarly, and in line with other emerging economies, doing business in South Africa requires the nimble negotiation of both formal and informal institutional structures and processes, not least because of a lack of coherence to formal institutional mechanisms (Mthant and Ojah, 2017) which, when set against the fragmented nature of South African business, creates a challenging environment within which firms must operate (ibid), leaving considerable scope for informal institutions to play an important role in business dealings.

As a particular emphasis is placed in this research on the informal and quasi-formal institutional practices that often characterise the 'real economy' of China, the majority of the following investigation will focus on how South African business actors comprehend, navigate and negotiate the Chinese institutional maze through their business strategies and networking activities. The contextual nature of the research subject therefore necessitates drawing further disciplinary perspectives into the study, beyond IB, including Social, Cultural and Area Studies. Furthermore, given the people-centred and informal institutional focus of a large component of this study, a heavy emphasis is placed on qualitative method (particularly case studies) in the following research investigation.

The Institutional Approach in IB Studies

The following is a brief overview of what I shall call an 'institutional approach', how it applies to IB studies, and how I propose to operationalise this approach in the current research. Scholars from different study fields have defined institutions in various ways in order to understand how they function within economic, political and socio-cultural systems and settings (Aguilera and Grøgaard, 2019). Depending on the context and research agenda, and which strands of Institutional Theory are used to inform their research, IB scholars commonly engage with three institutional perspectives in their studies: New Institutional Economics (NIE), New Organizational Institutionalism (NOI) and Comparative Institutionalism (CI) (Hotho and Pedersen, 2012). Of the three perspectives, NIE has progressed most rapidly in terms of its recent incorporation within IB studies (Zimbauer, 2001; Silva-Rêgo and Figueira, 2019).

The major proponents of the NIE stance in international business include the Nobel Laureates Douglass North (1990a, 1990b, 1991, 1999, 2005) and Oliver Williamson (2000). Unlike mainstream economics, NIE places an emphasis on the embedded institutions of the prevailing business environment (Söderbaum, 1992). Douglass North characterises institutions as the 'rules of the game', and this has become the generally accepted definition across disciplines. By combining behavioural and transaction cost theories in his research work, North (1990a) explained how formal rules, their enforcement mechanisms and various informal constraints in combination provide a set of institutional frameworks that regulate and stabilise the economic, political and social structures of a society. North (ibid.) differentiates 'organisations' from 'institutions': the former are the 'participants in the game' whilst the latter set the rules to which actors are expected to conform. In any scenario the participating organisations have to compete with each other in pursuit of their own optimal profit or benefit, but they are willing to follow the 'rules' in the interest of 'reducing uncertainties', especially in a foreign business environment. At the same time, organisations also evoke changes in institutions, although North suggests that such changes tend to be evolutionary and path-dependent (North, 1990a, 1991, 1999, 2005), and thus they also define the limits for individuals and organisations in terms of constricting their options or choices in various economic exchanges (North, 2005; Peng and Heath, 1996). The NIE approach takes it for granted that institutions are the 'constraints' that firms have to overcome by playing the game according to the rules. Within the international business environment, institutions may vie for influence: for instance, Ozawa (2005) has shown how MNEs from the United States, coming from one institutional environment, have influenced the evolution of institutions in the Japanese business sector.

Within the NIE, growing attention is being given to the role of institutions in business activities in emerging country markets (Peng, 2003, 2017; Ozawa, 2005; Jansson, 2007; Dunning and Lundan, 2008b; Silva-Rêgo and Figueira, 2019). Nonetheless, Dunning and Lundan (2008a, 125) suggest that much of the associated literature has tended to focus far more on formal institutional relations than the role played by informal institutions. The NIE approach also tends to emphasise state-level institutions, but downplays the everyday actions of individual firms which go 'beyond the rules of the game' (Hotho and Pedersen, 2012). Accordingly, there is a lack of consistent analysis between *macro-level* (state-level) factors and *micro-level* (firm-level) factors. The *agents* (such as financial organisations, labour unions) that exist between the *state* and the *market* create a series of *meso-level* institutions which help to maintain functional interactions between *state* and *market*, as well as bridging the gap between *macro-level* and *micro-level* institutions. This was indicated in Jansson's (2007) Institutional Network Approach which introduced three basic models: a *basic institutions model*, a *basic networks model*, and a *basic rules model*. These models formed a set of theoretical templates to explain the embedded networks between MNCs, markets and FDI host/home countries (states*)*. In addition, in their award-winning article, a research by Meyer and Peng (2005) on Central and East European firms first highlighted the role of *institution-based strategies* and was rightly lauded for contextualising institutions in IB research (Kostova and Hult, 2016).

NOI is another strand of institutional studies that has been engaged by IB scholars, with its key proponents being Richard Scott (1987, 2001, 2014) and Dimaggio and Powell (1983, 1991). Scott's perspective is somewhat different from that of North. He looks at institutions from a sociological perspective and draws attention to the role of organisations in institutional dynamics. Scott argues that organisations should be considered 'institutional forms' (Scott, 1987) which collectively are influenced by and adapted to their broader institutional arenas or contexts (Scott, 2001, 18). Scott (ibid., 48) sees institutions as consisting of three components: regulative, normative and cultural-cognitive. Based on his 'three pillars' framework, Scott later in this work introduces two further institutional concepts, carriers and levels, which are complementary to his analytical framework. The institutional carriers (symbolic systems, relational systems, routines and artefacts) perform as medium itinerants among different levels of institutions (world system, society, organisational field, organisational population, organisation and organisational subsystem), each of which can be explained and denoted from the three institutional components that make up Scott's 'three pillars'. These elements identified by Scott reflect the nature of institutions being both embedded and multi-faceted, and operating at multiple levels. Scott's sociological perspective views organisations as institutional forms which interact with the broader institutional structures and systems and act as 'institutional carriers' which connect different levels of institutions. Institutional transaction costs (i.e. the cost to a firm of overcoming problems and challenges associated with the prevailing institutional environment, both formal and informal) are suggested by Orr and Scott (2008) as a significant element of total transaction costs. In contrast to the NIE, the NOI approach tends to focus attention on the context of an individual nation's institutional environment, and acknowledge the impacts faced by MNCs as a result of the institutional distance between the home and host countries. Nonetheless, NOI research still focuses on state-level institutions and is less nimble when dealing with the complexity of local-level institutional contexts and any tensions which exist between the internal and external institutional environments (Hotho and Pedersen, 2012; Rana and Morgan, 2019).

A third strand of institutional theory is Comparative Institutionalism (CI) which emanates from Political Science. Although this approach also largely deals with state-level institutions, CI nonetheless shifts the emphasis towards sub-national (meso-)level institutions, and seeks to explain how MNCs respond to the socio-economic differences that exist between countries (Hotho and Pedersen, 2012). CI research relies heavily on case studies, and thus one criticism that is often levelled at CI is its context-specificity and associated impediments to theoretical generalisation. Early studies within CI were focused on seeking to explain the constraining and differentiating role of institutions in economic dynamics and efficiency within different developed market contexts (Whitley and Kristensen, 1996; Whitley, 1999). More recently, one variant of CI research, the National Business System (NBS) (Hotho, 2014; Rana and Morgan, 2019), has shifted the IB focus towards the capacities and capabilities of business firms as the core force in navigating the institutional environment, which is seen as both a constraining and enabling factor in business performance.

Institutions Operationalised: Applying an Institutional Approach to This Study

The following discussion will seek to operationalise the concept of 'institution' for the purposes of the present study. As we have seen, North (1990a) has defined institutions as the 'rules of a game' in which organisations participate. According to such a conception, institutions provide a general (macro) structure within which we can analyse the decisions and actions of actors, the relationships between them, and the consequences of these actions in different contextual settings (Kinra and Kotzab, 2008). This present research study investigates business relationships between two developing countries, but given that institutions are multifaceted, embedded and both durable and malleable social structures (Scott, 2001), we propose a multi-dimensional framework for understanding how institutions influence business activities in such a context, and how organisations navigate the prevailing institutional landscape.

The first dimension in defining institutions is based on the principle that organisations authorise and exercise different degrees of power over others, and this is often organised hierarchically from the macro, through meso- to the micro-levels (see Figure 2.1). Firm-level (micro) institutions, including firm managerial and operating systems, corporate governance and corporate culture, as well as everyday business practices, are influenced by and interact with the other two levels of institutions. Macro-level institutions refer to nation/state-level organisations and institutional practices consisting of political, economic and legal systems, the education/training system, all wrapped up in a country's official language, ideology, culture, customs and norms, religion, etc. These macro-level institutional arrangements are most typically manifest as national policies and the institutional mechanisms to implement these. In between these two levels, firms (micro) and state (macro) are linked through many intermediary (meso-level) institutions. These are typically made up of provincial and city regulatory systems, which in the main are influenced, directed and overseen from above, but which can – in some contexts more than others – be subject to local interpretation and manipulation. These meso-level institutions may in turn be influenced by local contextual variables, such as local dialect, customs and conventions, as well as structures of power, and define the context within which local firms operate, providing a bridge between the macro- and micro-levels. However, as we will discuss in the following sections, the influence of contextual variables determines that there are a great many institutional factors and processes which do not easily fit within this norma-tive macro/meso/micro framework.

Secondly, institutions from a normative perspective can also be loosely divided into formal institutions and informal institutions. According to Peng and Meyer (2011, 38), formal institutions are "laws, regulations and rules that are set by the authorised bodies", whilst informal institutions are "not formalised but still exist" in our societies. This phrase at first sight might appear somewhat vague and obvious, but the key point of Peng's statement is that we should not be bound by convention by restricting our enquiry solely to formal or 'conventional' institutions. In developed western coun-tries, societies are ordered and maintained by laws and regulations, but informal institutions (which may function to ease constraints provided by formal institutions, but which in turn may also constrain these same institu-tions), although on a small scale, can also have an impact on people's daily lives (North, 1999). In the developing world, informal institutions play a more influential role in various societal activities, especially during busi-ness interactions, and to a certain extent informal institutions may not nec-essarily be considered as constraints but may in fact mitigate uncertainties caused by formal institutions (Sautet, 2005).

Institutions have become a trendy topic that is increasingly being applied in business studies, as has been discussed earlier in this chapter. Increasingly, the role played by informal institutions in the wider institutional matrix is also something that both Business Studies and International Political Economy (IPE) have recognised as important in business dealings, most particularly in emerging country markets, such as China (Story, 2010). How might we define and operationalise the term 'informal institutions'? Whereas formal institutions are typically rule-based, informal institutions may be viewed as norm-based. Indeed, Wang (2000, 533) goes as far as to suggest that there are no formal rules (or at best a façade of formal rule-making) in informal institutional prac-tices (see also Williamson, 2009, 374). Instead, business actors operate along very fluid and flexible lines guided, or constrained, mainly by the normative limits imposed by a particular society. One such norm, for instance, might be reciprocity: drawing upon the social capital that may derive from informal business or social networks (Putnam, 2000), a business actor may call upon some form of assistance in order to progress their business interests, perhaps as a means of fast-tracking a business opportunity or stacking the cards in their favour, or overcoming the inefficiency of formal institutions or the actor's exclusion from them. Personal assistance thus obtained through informal chan-nels is more likely to be reciprocated (by returning a favour at some unspeci-fied but acknowledged point in the future) than compensated (in the shape of a formal financial transaction) by the receiver to the provider of assistance (Williamson, 2000, 534). Reciprocity thus ensures mutual benefit between parties, even though this may be far from even if measured in conventional ways (power and status also come into play here), and returns may not in the least be immediate (Yang, 1994). Indeed, network-building may in many instances be (or appear to the outside observer to be) speculative – a social investment made in the hope rather than the expectation of a longer-term financial (or other) return.

Trust is an important lubricant of informal institutional arrangements, and, again underwritten by prevailing social and cultural norms, may both derive from and provide the basis for developing the social networks which are a key manifestation of informal institutions in developing and transitional countries. Such networks may be extant, in the sense that an actor plugs into pre-existing social/familial/territorial networks, or may be carefully built and nurtured, perhaps with business utility in mind. Trust may in fact be built up through the normal operation of social networks, and may be easily broken where obligations and expectations are not met according to social norms. Serendipity may also play a role in the operational effectiveness of networks and contacts in a business sense: an actor may chance upon a relationship that works very effectively for their purposes; equally, 'investments' (gift-giving, patronage, meals and drinks, clubbing, sexual services, spa treatments, etc.) may be made but the returns may be sub-optimal. It is their fluid, unpredictable and contingent or contextual nature that helps to define 'informal institutions'. Informal institutional practices will be further discussed in the specific context of China in section 2.2.

Thirdly, an important institutional dimension lies at the interface of internal business structures and the institutional environment within which businesses function (we will call this the 'environmental perspective'). Internal institutions can be simply summarised as the institutional arrangements and practices within the firm, which may be specific to the firm or moulded by convention, or some combination of the two. They are generated within companies and have a direct impact on business, and in general they are controlled by the company although they may follow similar industry-specific patterns or conventions. Such institutional factors include the corporate business objective, value system, management structure and nature, internal power relations, human resources and other intangible equities, as well as the tangible assets of the firm. In contrast, external institutions refer to those institutions outside firms which may have an indirect influence on business, and usually these institutions are out of the firm's control. Impacts brought by these institutions could come from either those macro-level external environments (such as a country's political, legal, social and economic systems) or from those narrower levels of institutions which, because of operational proximity, normally have closer relationships and connections with local firms compared to the macro-level external institutions:

meso-level external institutions which may be made up of the institutional structures and practices that over time have been created, *inter alia*, by suppliers and customers, competitors, marketing intermediaries and financiers, etc. (Krapež *et al.*, 2012).

In this section we have briefly reviewed, from a theoretical perspective, how institutional theories have been incorporated into international business studies to offer explanations for how and to what effect MNCs penetrate and operate within host nations, highlighting that the way we understand the environment within which MNCs conduct business activities has changed over the last two or three decades. Building on the common ground of the three major institutional approaches, we distil the real-world complexity of institutional practice into three structural layers: macro (state-level, which includes both home and host country and requires rationalisation of any difference between the two), meso (cultural-normative or contextual, and includes both formal and informal institutional dynamics) and micro (firm-level contextual environment, which includes both internal and external institutional norms and practices). The core elements of the above discussion have been drawn upon in establishing a framework within which to conduct a multi-dimensional institutional analysis of South African FDI in China, where business, international relations, political and economic as well as sociological and cultural factors have been included.

2.2 The Chinese Institutional Environment for South African Investment

China joined the World Trade Organization in 2001, and since then has at least on paper been obliged to play the economic game according to international rules. In practice, there continue to be a number of 'distortions' which often frustrate or infuriate foreign firms seeking to enter and operate within the Chinese markets. As we shall see later in the case studies, one such contentious issue is China's lack of respect for and compliance with international standards on intellectual property protection. On a slightly more legitimate tack, but still serving the same ends, the Chinese government has also used joint ventures with foreign firms as a mechanism for gaining access to much-needed external technology (Redding and Witt, 2008, 6). Another gripe is the perceived lack of a level business 'playing field', with anecdotes rife among the ex-patriate business community in China concerning seemingly arbitrary decisions by officials to revoke business licences or sequester land and property – a situation which clearly does little to engender trust in the system and a sense of investment and operational security. To a significant degree, foreign firms quickly learn to put up with such uncertainties and institutionalised distortions because of the sheer size and potential of the Chinese domestic market, their sense (if not understanding) of the idiosyncrasies of the Chinese system, and their weighing up of the benefits of being on the inside despite the headaches experienced as opposed to missing out entirely on the China bonanza.

2.2.1 Formal Institutions in China

Macro-Level Institutions

Compared with foreign firms from advanced western countries, South African firms were relatively late-comers to the Chinese markets, since most did not arrive in China until the late 1990s. According to one of my interviewees, South African investors had found the 'big [i.e. state-level] environment' of China to be generally welcoming to their late involvement, but they complained that practical operations tended to be quite complex at lower administrative levels. Whilst the literature tends to view the Chinese market – at least that with which foreign firms and capital engage – as somewhat uniform and amorphous, the reality is that there are multiple layers, not least of regulatory administration, with which more or less all firms have to contend (Voss, 2011). At the macro-level, the principal actors that command direct authority to foreign inward investment include the State Council, the National Development and Reform Commission (NDRC), the Ministry of Commerce (MOFCOM), the State Administration for Industry and Commerce (SAIC), the People's Bank of China (PBC), the State Administration for Foreign Exchange (SAFE), the State Administration of Taxation (SAT) and the General Administration of Customs of the PRC (GACC). Other formal institutions must be navigated by investment projects which involve specific industries, although the State Council exercises overall regulatory power over all of these.

STATE COUNCIL

The State Council of China, also known as the Central People's Government, is the highest executive organ of state power and administration. The State Council, led by the Premier, is granted supreme power by the National People's Congress (NPC) and its Standing Committee, and is responsible for 'carrying out the principles and policies of the Communist Party of China as well as the regulations and laws adopted by the NPC" (www.gov. cn). The State Council performs as the highest administrative leadership unit, and functions as the supreme executor of administrative legislation, evaluating proposals, managing and monitoring the economic, diplomatic and social affairs of the State. All other state actors are subject to the State Council's oversight.

NATIONAL DEVELOPMENT AND REFORM COMMISSION

The NDRC is a successor to the State Development Planning Commission (SDPC), which was merged with the State Council Office for Restructuring the Economic System (SCORES) and part of the State Economic and Trade Commission (SETC) in 2003 (http://en.ndrc.gov.cn/mfndrc/). As one vital component of the government system, the major function of the NDRC is to macro-control the overall economic reform process, to provide guidance to economic restructuring by formulating and carrying out the state's economic and social development policies and to monitor macroeconomic development trends. The responsibility that the NDRC takes in regard to inbound foreign investment is to conduct and review feasibility studies, grant approval to foreign investment projects, and to guide and supervise the utilisation of foreign capital. Historically, the NDRC gave priority to projects that helped China secure much-needed natural resources, technology-transfer, improving in-firm management capacity and enhancing scope for export trade (Voss, 2007, 59). Decisions were also often prioritised according to the amount of inward investment, thereby giving greater emphasis to larger corporations than smaller SMEs.

MINISTRY OF COMMERCE

MOFCOM is an iteration of the former Ministry of Foreign Trade and Economic Co-operation (MOFTEC), following a restructuring in 2003, and shares a similar function to the NDRC with regard to foreign investment matters. In terms of inbound foreign investment, the major missions of MOFCOM are: (i) to draft and enforce laws and regulations governing foreign investment activities nationwide in China, as well as to establish guidance for the drafting of lower level administrative rules and regulations for foreign investment management; (ii) to examine and approve, usually in conjunction with the NDRC, inward foreign direct investment, as well as to monitor large-scale foreign invested projects, in terms both of their stated objectives and feasibility and also their compliance and success; and (iii) to provide regulatory guidance to investment promotion agencies (IPA) at all levels, as well as supervising the work of state-level special economic development zones (www.mofcom.gov.cn).

STATE ADMINISTRATION FOR MARKET REGULATION

State Administration for Market Regulation (SAMR) is a state institution at ministerial level and under the direct supervision of the State Council, which was newly created under the State Council Institutional Reform Program in March 2018. SAMR is an outcome of reshuffling several government bodies to streamline administrative regulations. SAMR merged several ministerial-level institutions, including the State Administration for Industry and Commerce (SAIC), Anti-Monopoly Bureau, Price Supervision, Standardized Administration of China, State Intellectual Property Office, etc. According to SAMR's official stipulation, the agency exercises comprehensive responsivities in 17 areas of market supervision and management (www.samr.gov.cn/jg/). For foreign investors, "the SAMR will essentially regulate the following functions: drug safety supervision; quality inspection; fair competition and commercial bribery; issuance of business registration; certification and accreditation; management of intellectual property rights; and comprehensive supervision and management of the market order" (Piat, 2018).

GENERAL ADMINISTRATION OF CUSTOMS (GACC), STATE ADMINISTRATION OF TAXATION (SAT), STATE ADMINISTRATION OF FOREIGN EXCHANGE (SAFE), THE STATE-OWNED ASSETS SUPERVISION AND ADMINISTRATION COMMISSION OF THE STATE COUNCIL (SASAC)

These three offices are the highest level of state administration managing customs, tax and foreign exchange affairs in China. In terms of the supervision of national monetary issues, the three administrations have different functions: GACC exercises customs control and revenue collection; SAT is responsible for tax collection; and SAFE is in charge of monitoring and supervising the foreign flow and exchange of the national currency, the RMB, as well as providing guidance and strategy suggestions for the People's Bank of China on foreign exchange policies. Regarding inbound FDI in the Chinese markets, foreign enterprises have to carry out registrations at the beginning of their business establishment at all levels (state, provincial and even city) with these administrative offices, by law. These administrative requirements may happen simultaneously, although because of a frequent lack of clarification on administrative procedures at every administrative level, the registration process tends to be operated sequentially and not necessarily in the most logical order, which can be time-consuming for newly established foreign enterprises, and may compromise their financial efficiency. SASAC is a special commission and directly led by the State Council. The institution was founded in 2003 through a process of consolidating various industry-specific ministries. The major responsibility of SASAC is to manage state-owned enterprises (SOEs), including appointing top executives and approving any mergers or sales of stock or assets, as well as drafting laws related to SOEs.

OTHERS

People's Bank of China (PBC), China Securities Regulatory Commission (CSRC), China Insurance Regulatory Commission (CIRC), China Banking Regulatory Commission (CBRC)

The PBC functions as China's central bank and is responsible for overall monetary policy-making and maintaining order in China's financial market. In the past 30 years of dealing with inward foreign direct investment, the PBC has formulated and advanced a policy to control and manage capital utilisation by foreign enterprises. The promulgated operational rules of RMB account settlement for foreign investment, introduced in 2012, was an important clarification by the PBC of the procedures regulating capital flows across mainland China's borders. The CSRC, CIRC and CBRC are three typical monetary agencies that are directly authorised by the State Council to be in charge of the security market and the insurance industry respectively. CIRC and CBRC merged into CBIRC in 2018, again following the institutional reforms, with the aim to eliminate any cross-regulatory vagueness in business transactions. Foreign invested enterprises that are involved in such industries – as with two of my case study firms – have to abide by the rules and regulations stipulated by the CSRC or CBIRC (China Banking and Insurance and Regulatory Commission), on top of the administrative procedures specified above. The formal, state-level institutional environment in China is therefore quite complex, but the position of the State Council at the apex of this formal institutional pyramid illustrates the extent to which the central government asserts political control over the operations of each and every one of these formal financial institutions.

Beyond listing the main macro-level formal institutions that have relevance and importance for South African firms entering the Chinese markets, we need also to gain a feel for how they function and whether, on balance, they help to facilitate or complicate market entry. Whilst the array and layers of formal institutions in China is impressive verging on intimidating, their principal function – at least in relation to inward foreign direct investment, which is a typical channel for foreign firms entering the Chinese markets – is strategic more than it is facilitatory. The Chinese government uses four Catalogues for Guidance on Foreign Investment Projects (CGFIP) to determine where inward investment should be encouraged or discouraged, and this influences the priorities set by the highly influential State Council which are then mirrored in other formal institutions (Davies, 2012, 5). The 'prohibited' catalogue (category) specifies those economic sectors and spatial locations where foreign investment is not allowed (OECD, 2008). The 'restricted' catalogue allows investment but under a quite strict and often time-consuming regime of scrutiny, approvals and evaluations (ibid.).

Included in this category are several economic sectors which China was obliged to open up following its accession to the WTO in 2001, but which it has managed to retain some control over through its CGFIP system (Davies, 2012, 5). Reflecting, therefore, the political orchestration of formal economic institutions, there is also mounting pressure from domestic firms to place more restrictions on foreign invested firms in order to ease the competition that they currently experience in the home and international markets from foreign firms that have become established in China. In contrast, the 'permitted' and 'encouraged' categories promise (but don't always deliver) increasingly higher levels of support and facilitation by Chinese formal institutions as the country seeks to steer investment away from the overheating coastal provinces into the interior, and towards key economic sectors where China still lags in terms of international competitiveness, including high technology and greener production processes (ibid.).

Meso-Level Institutions

Meso-level institutions which, naturally, stand between those at the macro- and micro-levels function to coordinate and lubricate the relationship between state-level and local-level institutions, and, at least in theory, to mitigate disconnections or conflicts between the two (see the following sections). In the context of inward foreign investment, meso-level institutions provide a platform and mechanism for foreign enterprises to facilitate, enlarge and bridge their existing (and, as the case studies show, often quite limited) institutional networks at the local level, whilst also channelling feedback on business practices and needs to higher level institutions in order to help refine and advance business and economic policy.

Micro-Level Institutions

Apart from the State Council, NDRC and PBC, the remainder of state administrations and agencies all have affiliates at the local level, i.e. at provincial and city levels. Although the local affiliates abide by the guidance given by the state administrations, the local authorities are allowed and obliged to introduce their own sub-regulations and rules according to the needs of the local development context. This accordingly has led to deeply embedded and often quite complicated (layers of) institutional mechanisms for foreign invested enterprises to follow in the Chinese markets. Figure 2.1 is a simplified indication of the connections and supervisory relationships between the state- and local-level administrations within the Chinese institutional environment governing investment.

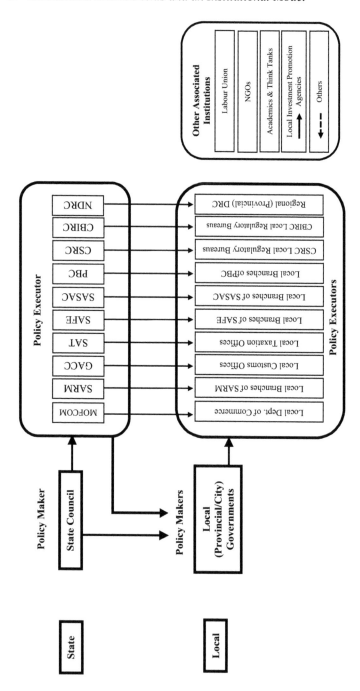

Figure 2.1 Structure of Formal Institution in the People's Republic of China

Whilst the chart suggests a structured and seamless functional integration of institutions at all levels, the reality in China is often quite different, a fact that has quite significant implications for foreign-invested firms that venture beyond the main centres of economic activity and outside the realm of formal state-level institutions. An interesting article by Krug and Hendrischke (2008) and a journalistic piece by Wu (2006) provide some useful insight in this regard. A by-product of the reform process has been a relative weakening of central government control over local-level decision-making and action-taking. Gone[2] are the days of 'strongman politics' (e.g. Mao Zedong taking the country in one direction, Deng Xiaoping steering it towards its present situation) under the centralised command economy (Wu, 2006), which in the post-reform era has been replaced by a decentralised politics in which local officials defy diktats from Beijing with increasing levels of confidence. Wu gives the example of how one of the formal institutions introduced above, the NDRC, has since 2004 sought to close down large numbers of iron and steel works and coal mines at the local level because of fears of overproduction, pollution and worker safety, only to have its orders ignored by local governments who do not wish to lose important revenue streams and jobs, and who fear local political ramifications:

> [s]ince economic activities take place at localities, they are directly linked to local interests. Local officials are eager to boost the local economy to show their performance in hope for promotion. They do not need and do not want to view things from the point of view of national interests. Thus it is natural that they would try to defend local interests when such interests are in conflict with national ones.
>
> (Wu, 2006, n.p.)

What this means from an institutional perspective is that the seemingly neat arrangement of layers of regulatory competence – a uniform institutional architecture (Krug and Hendrischke, 2008, 82) – masks a much more complex, contradictory and dysfunctional reality which, in turn, suggests a far-from-integrated market and anything but a single business system (ibid.). As we will see later in this chapter, the interface of business, politics and administration at the local level opens up huge scope for the functioning of informal institutional practices which, we argue, and as the three-dimensional institutional model to be presented at the end of this chapter suggests, are in many instances more important and influential than the formal institutional environment that is being described here.

Section 2.2, to this point, has touched on the functionality of formal institutions affecting foreign enterprises' business strategies. As we have seen above, the complicated institutional environment within which foreign invested enterprises are embedded in China is sometimes quite cumbersome and confusing: each administrative body and layer has regulatory responsibility on paper, but the permutations and manifestations of power for executing these responsibilities are complex and far from uniform. In such circumstances, it is perhaps unavoidable that these firms encounter and experience hindrances and impediments when they enter, operate and seek to consolidate their position within the Chinese markets due to the ambiguity of the institutional landscape that confronts them and their own lack of local knowledge as to how to negotiate this landscape. In order to compensate for their shortcomings in this regard, many foreign enterprises engage local actors and agents to help them steer a path through this institutional minefield, and it is here that informal channels often open up to these foreign firms as the most effective means to overcome obstacles and both accelerate and smooth their business development path.

2.2.2 Informal Institutions in China

I will finish this section by looking at informal institutional practices in China which, almost inevitably, centre on the phenomenon of *guanxi*, which is the most central and most commonly discussed informal institution in China. Discussion will focus on the character, source, operation and importance of *guanxi*, and how it is institutionalised.

What Is Guanxi?

Lucian Pye (1992, 101) has described *guanxi* as "friendship with implications of continued exchange of favors". It is thus social relationships which carry reciprocal obligations once the relationship has been deployed in a way that bestows favours or advantages to one or more parties (Tsang, 1998, 65). The word *guanxi* literally means 'relationship' or 'connection' in Chinese, which implies both that it is built upon people's personal connections which are structured as social networks, but also that there is a social dynamic or 'relationship' component which holds these networks together. Because of its instrumental value, *guanxi* can be likened to social capital (Putnam, 2000), being simultaneously a 'social glue' which binds networks together and a 'business lubricant' which eases transactions within them.

It is quite common to see *guanxi* in China described as a universal and homogeneous entity, but I think this is unhelpful (a point that has some significance when shortly we turn to consider how foreign firms negotiate China's socio-cultural landscape). First, it is important to emphasise that China itself is a remarkably diverse nation, made up of a myriad of ethnic groups, a heterogeneous landscape, a fragmented and far from untroubled history, and quite extreme differences in the level of economic development and transformation, thus even to consider that there may be uniform cultural practices across this diverse human landscape must be problematic. Second, *guanxi* is better seen as a generic 'umbrella' under which a heterogeneous variety of social, cultural, political and economic practices takes, such as in business, gift-giving, entertaining, inviting people on trips, using intermediaries to establish contacts, in addition to its more traditional familial functions (Zhang and Zhang, 2006, 379).

Another set of structural factors is also argued to lie behind the imperatives – or the 'why' – of the *guanxi* system. According to Tsang (1998), the hierarchical nature of Chinese society across time has typically determined that resources and the decision-making over the allocation of resources have not been fairly and evenly distributed, but have remained in the hands of powerful individuals and, more latterly, state institutions. *Guanxi* has been used by people to gain access to these resources, to influence allocations decisions and to gain information which may give them an advantage (or reduce their disadvantage) in this regard (ibid., 65). Concurrently, while the influential members of society could use their power over allocation decisions to enhance their own social standing, the socio-cultural 'rules of the game' (to which we will return shortly) set limits between the use and the abuse of power in this regard. As such, parallels can be drawn between *guanxi* and patron-clientship as social systems: neither is a one-way street. Across time, it has been the shortcomings of formal institutional arrangements in distributing resources and opportunities fairly, evenly and efficiency which has created functional and instrumental space for informal social practices to achieve the same ends, although, as we shall see shortly, *guanxi* networks can be exclusionary as well as inclusionary.

Where Does Guanxi Come From?

The crucial building-blocks of *guanxi* are people and their social relationships. But interactions between people have many facets, and relationships may take many forms. Thus, it is important to signal different types of *guanxi* according to the actors who are involved in the associated networks. We can, for instance, identify what is called 'artefactual *guanxi*' (Dunfee and Warren, 2001, 196), which may consist of pre-existing *guanxi* relationships into which one is born and over which one has limited agency, for example that which exists within nuclear and extended families, and clans. Other *guanxi* is 'acquired' or 'achieved' through social interaction and social investment (Tsang, 1998, 65; Dunfee and Warren, 2001, 192). Friendships, for instance, are established through the course of life, usually through choice but often also through circumstances. In China, some of the most influential friends in *guanxi* networks are former school and particularly university classmates, and also workmates. This helps explain why parents often invest so much financial and emotional energy in getting their children into the best educational establishments, through which they are more likely to meet the next generation of influential citizens. But simply meeting someone at university or being an alumnus of the same university as someone who is later encountered in the business setting is not, in itself, a sufficient ingredient of *guanxi*. According to Tsang (1998, 66), a very important additional factor is *ganqing* or 'affection'. In other words, a relationship must have a degree of closeness and emotional commitment to be able to function as *guanxi*, and to allow the parties to make reciprocal demands upon one another. Thus, *ganqing* might be seen as the social lubricant of *guanxi* networks, goodwill underwritten by sincerity, which takes time to be nurtured. It also helps to explain why not all Chinese can deploy *guanxi* to the same extent in all instances: personality is an important ingredient of *ganqing*, and personalities either 'gel' (*yijian rugu*) or they do not (ibid., 66). Nonetheless, coming from the 'right' family or business background helps some relationships to gel more readily than others.

But there are other essential ingredients to *guanxi* that also serve to underwrite the social networks and the functions they play. Trust, integrity and reputational credibility are simultaneously indispensable components and vital products of *guanxi* (Fan, 2007, 502–503), particularly in formal institutional, political, legal and social settings which – perhaps because of corruption or rent-seeking, bureaucratic inefficiency, or social exclusion – fail to engender confidence, trust and accessibility from everyday citizens (Lovett *et al.*, 1999; Dunfee and Warren, 2001, 197). Informal and interpersonal social mechanisms substitute for formal institutional failures. Trust may be primordial within the family setting (Tsang, 1998, 65), but needs to be built and maintained in other social situations. Typically, in China and the Chinese diaspora, trust must be built up before a business relationship can be cemented (Hwang *et al.*, 2009, 236), and thus there is often considerable investment in socialising – meals, drinks, entertainment, trips – before the topic of business is formally addressed (Peng *et al.*, 2008). Social interaction will also continue throughout the business relationship, not just occur at its outset. Gifts will periodically be exchanged as part of this process – a form of etiquette (Carlisle and Flynn, 2005, 83) – although gift-giving has more recently become seriously constrained by the Chinese government's recent strict anti-corruption measures. Time is an important factor in *guanxi* relationships, allowing *ganqing* to mature: the Chinese have a saying that 'an old friend is better than just a friend' (Tsang, 1998, 68). Once the parties feel that they have a foundation of trust, confidence and credibility – where simply one's word rather than a written contract can become the basis of a business transaction – the business partnership itself becomes part of the process of building and maintaining trust. Partners will be reluctant to default on loans, or fail to deliver materials on time, or create other problems and impediments as these will erode the trust and confidence that is felt between the two parties. At the same time, this trust-based business relationship will help to reduce transaction costs and uncertainty, thereby yielding mutually beneficial advantages to both parties in the business relationship.

Guanxi may also be transferable (Tsang, 1998, 65), hence the notion of 'bridging social capital' (Larsen *et al.*, 2004) whereby a third party may plug into an existing network, although usually only if this is carefully mediated by one party or another, and follows clear protocols. This aspect is also relevant to the case of foreign firms doing business in China, and thus will be returned to later in this section.

How Important Is Guanxi?

The instrumental value of *guanxi* is perhaps best gauged not so much in absolute terms but relative to the context within which it functions. Thus, if the rule of law is clear, trusted, efficient and fair, the use of *guanxi* to underwrite business agreements (or contracts) may appear to be superfluous, or perhaps even counterproductive. If government exists to serve the interests of the business community, as opposed to the interests of the state (more typical of modern China, as discussed earlier), with strong and efficient formal institutions designed to assist every stage of the business process, then the use of *guanxi* networks to seek out information and to clear bureaucratic hurdles would again appear to be redundant or even pointless. The importance of context to the character and utility of *guanxi* is one reason why the nature and importance of *guanxi* is not the same in mainland China as in many overseas Chinese communities, Singapore for instance, where formal institutions function well and the continued reliance on *guanxi* in China is frowned upon: the late Singapore Prime Minister Lee Kwan Yew is reported once to have said that the Chinese use *guanxi* "to make up for the lack of the rule of law and transparency in rules and regulations" (Dunfee and Warren, 2001, 197).

But in China, where there are still substantial acknowledged weaknesses in the formal institutional environment, as we have discussed earlier in this chapter, *guanxi* continues, and will continue, to play a vital role. In the business context, *guanxi* is typically important in the pursuit of new customers and the maintenance of a company's customer base; in smoothing business operations and ensuring the timely delivery of resources and materials; in obtaining investment capital; and charting a path through government bureaucracy (Dunfee and Warren, 2001, 193) and the sometimes seemingly arbitrary decisions or interventions of government (Carlisle and Flynn,

2005, 84). *Guanxi* is particularly important for business firms which do not already have a direct link to government officials, given the number of bureaucratic procedures and hurdles that a business will typically encounter during its establishment and routine functioning – approvals, licencing, inspections, taxation, compliance with regulations, etc. (Gomez-Arias, 1998; Peng *et al.*, 2008; Tsang, 1998, 67; Davies *et al.*, 1995).

It is important to emphasise that *guanxi* has both negative and positive connotations. A respondent to a survey by Tung and Worm (1997, 11) indicated that the best form of *guanxi* "is where I've got something on you" – in other words, the *guanxi* relationship was asymmetrical (as with a patron and client situation), where one party for some reason or other was obligated to the other, who could then use this fact to their strategic advantage, or, in a more sinister sense, in a situation which was not far removed from blackmail. There has also been considerable debate (e.g. Dunfee and Warren, 2001; Su and Littlefield, 2001; Hwang *et al.*, 2009) about the ethics of *guanxi*. Given the fact that it is typically deployed in a secretive, tacit and verbal manner to find a route around bureaucratic procedures or through regulatory minefields, to secure competitive advantages in the business field and to fast-track personal interests ahead of those of others, added to the prominence of gift-giving and other forms of 'lubrication' as a key *modus operandi*, it is understandable why it is often difficult to draw a clear distinction between *guanxi* and corruption. However, the link between *guanxi* and corruption might possibly be spurious, or at least tangential: "it is the deficiency in China's institutional framework that not only leads to the negative effect of Guanxi practice but also introduces bribery and corruption into it" (Zhang and Zhang, 2006, 378).

How Is Guanxi Institutionalised?

We have seen earlier in this chapter that institutions are defined as the rules by which people play, in this instance on the transnational business playing field. But one thing that distinguishes formal institutions from informal institutions is the clear organisational structure and clearly defined rules and regulations of the former, and the seemingly chaotic, almost anarchic character of the latter. This section suggests this to be an inaccurate characterisation. The weakness of this caricature lies in the tendency to see the formal and the informal as diametric opposites: the latter lacks everything that the former possesses. In reality, as the above discussion has already intimated, both sets of institutions have their own rules, norms, values and boundaries (and both have their rule-breakers, unethical actors, norms-ignorers and boundary-transgressors). The following sub-section will attempt to pull out from the earlier discussion those elements that serve to 'institutionalise' informal business practices.

Circumstances, combinations, needs, temporality and, most certainly, personality create seemingly unique permutations in the character and functionality of *guanxi*. But at the same time, everyone who is building and using *guanxi* in China knows what it is, knows how it works, knows where the limits are set, and is aware of the risks associated with ignoring its tacit rules. We have seen that trust is an essential ingredient of *guanxi*. I would add, from a personal viewpoint, that entering into a *guanxi* relationship arms one with the trust (or confidence) that the system will ensure that the other party will act according to the established rules and norms of *guanxi*. This is particularly important in the era of the market economy in China because of the competitive environment it has engendered, and the acquisitive culture it has spawned. As such, we could argue that it is the institutional elements of *guanxi* that help to hold society together, defining the values and limits of individual action, rather than *guanxi* simply existing as a means of helping people to chart a path through a dysfunctional society against an anarchic failure of formal institutions. I think there is an important distinction between these two perspectives.

Guanxi relationships are often underwritten by a sense of obligation (*renqing*). The institutionalised rules, set against the Chinese cultural context, dictate that there are many things that parties have to do, even if ideally they would not want to do them. The Chinese seasonal festivals provide a useful illustration: at least three times each year (New Year, Spring Festival, Mid-Autumn Festival) employers, clients, business partners and senior family members are expected to demonstrate generosity through bestowing gifts (e.g. mooncakes during the Mid-Autumn Festival) on other people in their social and business networks. The larger the organisation the more complex and time-consuming a task this is. For some of the larger companies, the entire Human Resources department will spend weeks, perhaps even months, ensuring that the right gifts are sent to the right clients. Failure to remember and acknowledge a client or partner in this way will risk causing offence, which in turn will risk jeopardising the business relationship. Against the backdrop of the market economy, with more and more wealth available and visible, gift-giving as the currency of *guanxi* almost ran out of control, with partners either seeking to outdo each other with ever more lavish gifts, or fearing that a lesser level of extravagance would send the wrong signals to the other party. The tacit rules of *guanxi*, which form part of its institutionalisation, risked running out of control when wrapped up in an evolving Chinese consumerist culture until the central government under Xi Jinping cracked down heavily on corruption, at the same time severely curtailing the extent to which individuals and businesses could use financial generosity, even profligacy, to lubricate *guanxi* relationships.

This brings us to a wider question of how the institution of *guanxi*, the primordial informal institution in China, has changed with the country's evolving economic, social and political context. If we accept the deep historical and cultural roots of *guanxi*, and the purpose it served in the past, how and why is it still valid today, not least since the market reforms of 1979? As we saw at the beginning of this chapter, China has made steady progress in the reform of its formal institutions, not least since its accession to the World Trade Organization in 2001 and its associated acceptance of the need to operate according to international business standards (Guthrie, 1998). The private sector has steadily increased in size relative to the public sector, including many state-owned enterprises that have switched to private ownership. Business operation according to the logic of the market, with price competition and efficiency the main drivers of enhanced productivity, would logically leave less room for non-commercial actions and actors in the business environment. As business moves forward, Guthrie (ibid.) claims that social obligations start to become a liability rather than an asset. Spatial mobility interferes with *guanxi* networks, and requires the establishment of new relationships in new locations, which takes time. And yet the institution of *guanxi* shows little sign of weakening as a consequence. This is in part because formal institutional reform is only partial and incomplete: Nikkel (1995, 515) argues that *guanxi* continues to provide the main means of dispute arbitration, mediation and resolution because legal reforms have not yet delivered the certainty, fairness and efficiency that both Chinese and foreign business managers require. Lovett *et al.* (1999) go so far as to suggest that reliance on *guanxi* is in fact increasing as the country's economic transition has greatly outpaced and outstripped the capacity of formal institutions to perform efficiently and effectively. Business people still have more trust in *guanxi* than in formal legal contracts (Dunfee and Warren, 2001, 193).

Guanxi and Foreign Firms

Given its importance to the establishment of a client and customer base, the navigation of bureaucratic and administrative channels, and the day-to-day running of a business, how can foreign firms manage in the Chinese market if and when they come 'cold' to the Chinese institutional environment? This is a question that is best addressed by means of empirical case studies, and as such will provide one of the core research questions that will be addressed in the following chapter. But first I will raise a few pertinent questions in this regard.

The first question is whether different sets of rules might apply to Chinese and foreign-owned firms. Despite the apparently universal character and cultural-embeddedness of *guanxi*, perhaps there are niches where business practice is truly internationalised and operates according to acknowledged international standards and practices? It is here that foreign firms find an initial foothold in the Chinese marketplace? It is better to accept one's identity as a foreign firm than pretend too hard to be Chinese (Tsang, 1998, 70). Or perhaps allowances are made by Chinese counterparts for the fact that newcomers can hardly be expected to have initiated and matured *guanxi* networks at the point of entry into the market? There is a concept called '*sheng-ren guanxi*' which is the *guanxi* formed in the relationship between strangers (Su and Littlefield, 2001).

Perhaps too much emphasis is given to *guanxi* as a uniquely Chinese socio-cultural phenomenon, with insufficient allowance being made for the possibility that social networking and socialising for the purpose of enhancing business prospects are global universals which just have different names, natures and niches. Thus, on entering the Chinese market, business actors simply need to adjust and fine-tune their normal informal business practices. Perhaps insufficient recognition is given to the possibility that foreign business actors from some regions of the world – developing countries in particular – are already deeply familiar with the need to navigate and negotiate the impediments and inefficiencies of the formal institutional environment by means of informal institutional practices. This is a question we will address in the following chapter by looking at case studies of South African business actors operating in China.

Finally, perhaps the mode of entry into the Chinese market is the most important determinant of a company's awareness of and ability to handle the informal institutional channels along which much business activity operates. Joint ventures and joint capital arrangements, for instance, involve both foreign and Chinese counterparts, and one thing that the latter can contribute to the partnership is an existing array of *guanxi* networks plus a cultural understanding of the best ways to operate a business in the Chinese setting. Foreign firms may deploy or employ ethnic Chinese members of their own staff in order to deal with the cultural challenges of doing business in China, or may employ local Chinese staff for the same purpose. Or, quite typically, they may operate via agents who offer their own *guanxi* as an asset to help a foreign firm enter the market or find appropriate local partners for their business ventures. Once a foothold has become established, firms can then start to invest in building their own *guanxi* in order to consolidate their position in the Chinese market. This may give them a competitive edge over other foreign firms. Also, it is not uncommon for foreign firms to enter China – in the form of a Representative Office – many months or years before they inaugurate their business in that country, simply to allow them to build *guanxi* and cultural familiarity (Tsang, 1998, 70).

2.3 A Three-Dimensional (3D) Institutional Model

The institutional elements specified earlier in this chapter are mapped out in a three- dimensional institution model as shown in Figure 2.2 which describes four types of business scenarios (Cells I, II, III and IV) and four types of business transforming processes (Cells V, VI, VII and VIII), from which a firm's business strategies take specific advantage of various institutional arrangements. The left vertical axis represents the three-level institutional structure, and internal/external institutional interfaces (permutations of micro, meso and macro) are identified on the right vertical axis, whilst the horizontal axis stands for the two kinds of institutions from a normative perspective – the informal and formal institutions.

Cells II and III describe scenarios that businesses normally initiate and realise at higher levels of institutional environments, where firms are strictly regulated by macro-level institutions, and cannot directly control the impacts and constraints these institutions impose on them. However, the difference between the two business scenarios is that Cell II firms can mitigate certain uncertainties through the assistance of informal institutions, but Cell III firms cannot, and hence they can only abide by the rules of formal institutions. In business reality, if two firms from Cell II and Cell III are competitors in the same market, the degree of uncertainties for the Cell II

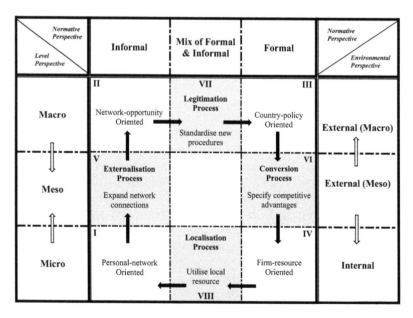

Figure 2.2 The Three-Dimensional (3D) Institutional Model

firm can be reduced to enable them to be more competitive in the market compared to the Cell III firm. But given the nature of informal institutions being personal and random, the Cell III firm can only realistically expect to be able to reduce (but not eliminate) the uncertainties, but even this may be beyond their reach. Therefore, the Cell II firms are in an opportunity-oriented business scenario, whilst Cell III firms are policy-oriented. Compared with Cells II and III, Cell I and Cell IV are two types of business situated at the lower level of institutional environments. Firms themselves have their own array of micro-level institutional arrangements, and thus have direct control over their general business, quickly creating new institutional arrangements and structures to respond to changing business situations. But firms can conduct very different business strategies if they fall into Cell I compared to those in Cell IV. Cell I represents a personal-network oriented business scenario, where firms generate new business opportunities or expand existing markets through enlarged personal interconnections and networks. Meanwhile, firms in Cell IV are most likely to rely on their own resources, so these types of business scenarios are firm-resource oriented.

Several points need to be clarified. Firstly, among the four types of business scenarios, there are no absolute criteria to use to judge whether one type is better than the others, or that firms falling into Type III have a better success rate than firms belonging to Type II. Each type of business scenario is a description of the major business strategy that drives the firms under a certain institutional environment and at one given moment in time. It could be the starting point of some new business, or the mature stage of one particular business operation. And secondly, the four types of business scenarios together form a certain business development cycle but this is largely a closed cycle: any scenario out of the four business types could be the point where firms start new business, but firms do not necessarily follow the order from Type I to IV (as we will see in Chapter 3). However, empirical research results do appear to indicate that there is a particular cyclical pattern that firms usually follow to develop their business. But before going into further detail about this it is essential to introduce the four types of business transforming and development processes.

Firms of each business scenario have their own specific competitive advantages over others, which is also the basic grounding on how firms design and utilise their business strategies. But as their business develops, the institutional environments where firms are based may also change. New business strategies are adopted to meet the firms' needs, and the process of firms adopting new strategies also enables them to transfer from one business scenario to the next. Each transforming process actually corresponds to the business strategies that the firms undertake to develop their business from one stage to the next.

Cell V is a transforming process to allow firms from Cell I to enlarge their existing local networks to higher levels, which could create more opportunities for business, which are enjoyed by firms from Cell III. This network-expanding process is termed the 'externalisation process'. Under the lower institutional environments, Cell I firms with limited resources could be assisted through personal networks to span relations with other people, but the people they are interacting with may be clustered under similar environments. The structure of such a network is rather thin and the information and resource provided to firms would be increasingly inadequate as their business grows. Compared to Cell I firms, Cell III firms have a more complicated network structure, which means such multi-layers of relationships and connections enable firms with wider sources to retain more valuable information and resource as well as shorten the paths or eliminate the burdens on the way to attaining their business targets (Scott, 1991; Burt, 1992; Hansen, 1995; Greve and Salaff, 2003). During the externalisation process, one major theme of Cell I firms' business strategies is to explore new channels to bridge wider relations and interactions with people who are outside their previous circles. The new relations and interactions will generally come from higher-level institutional environments and have closer connections with contacts associated with Cell III firms. This transforming process is highly driven by personal inter-connections and normally happens under informal contexts, so it is not a process requiring high enforcement to realise.

On the other side, Cell VI presents a transforming process to require Cell III firms to specify their firm-level competitive advantages so as to adapt themselves from positions where they might enjoy support or be constrained by the macro-level institutions to a situation where they have more self-control and initiative in their business through utilising their own resources, and this is the conversion process. From an institutional perspective, although Cell III firms are usually policy-controlled by higher-level institutions, institutions do not unilaterally restrain their business activities. Business opportunities and initiatives could stem from such an institutional environment for both foreign and domestic companies because of specific government policies made at certain time scales, and these opportunities would favour firms with certain country specific advantages (CSAs). In his early CSA/FSA matrix, Rugman (1981) suggested CSAs benefitting from host country and firms' own FSAs (firm specific advantages) emanating from the home country are two major building blocks to decide MNEs' competitiveness in the host country markets. But increasing foreign investments from developing countries have called for the evolution of traditional business frameworks. Rugman and Verbeke (2008; see also Rugman, 2008) discussing this issue have focused attention on CSAs emanating from the home region and their affective relations with FSA (Rugman *et al.*, 2011). Firms do not generate concrete profits in the Cell III scenario, because the environment only provides the rules of the game (namely the regulations and policies) but not a platform for the game, unless firms could specify their own FSAs which would enable them to utilise fully the home country CSAs and circumvent host country-specific disadvantages (CSDs), and to transform through a conversion process into Cell IV scenarios where firms can participate in the game with other rivals on the game platform – the market.

On the horizontal axis of Figure 2.2 there occur another two transmission processes. A legitimation process stems from the upper-level institutional structure (Cell VII). Theorists have observed that legitimacy has the nature of being normative and cognitive, and defining legitimacy has always been associated with institutions and organisations (Hybels, 1995; Suchman, 1995; Tilling, 2004). Hybels (1995, 241) pointed out that "social systems change over time and consist of multiple institutions. Thus, the institutionalisation of a feature of society derives from a legitimation process that occurs over time, and the legitimation process itself derives largely from institutions other than that being legitimated." In the 3D institutional model, firms in Cell II are proffered new business initiatives and information that generate new business opportunities, which are relatively rare resources for firms in other business scenarios (Cell I, III and IV) to attain. Like any organisation in the institutional structures, business organisations (Cell II firms) have to justify and attain approval from superior organisations (generally from state government level, but often mediated through meso-level institutions) for their relatively novel business behaviour. And only afterwards would such new procedures become standardised and be available for other late-comers. This is echoed by Hybels (1995) when he referred to Maurer's (1971) work, "Legitimation is the process whereby an organisation justifies to a peer or superordinate system its right to exist" (1971, 361); as well as Berger and Luckmann's (1967), "the function of legitimation is to make objectively available and subjectively plausible to 'first order' objectivations that have been institutionalised" (1967, 72).

Last but not least, the transition process in the 3D institutional model is a localisation process indicated in Cell VIII. It can be summarised as a series of actions that foreign managers have to take in the foreign markets by fully utilising local resources, in order to compensate for their own liabilities of foreignness (Hymer, 1960). From a traditional macro-level perspective, the host country's policy, infrastructure and resources, as well as market-size are the major locational factors that concern firms on their first entry into the market according to Dunning's OLI paradigm (Dunning, 1988). But with firm-specific assets becoming more mobilised and extending beyond physical boundaries over the last two decades, it is necessary to make some modifications to some earlier theoretical explanations (Dunning and Lundan, 2008b). The traditional location business theories might give guidance to MNEs (most from developed economies) to break into new markets, but new issues arriving with emerging country markets have challenged the classical locational choices of MNEs, because markets in these countries (such as China) reflect strong regional differences, which may create hindrances for businesses and managers, especially if they are unaware of the micro-level institutional environment and arrangements (Orr and Scott, 2008). Thus, the notion of 'going local' becomes an important business strategy for foreign firms operating in such markets.

The following discussion in Chapter 3 will explore the extent to which, and how, South African firms entering the Chinese market have managed to achieve localisation. During the localisation process, firms of Cell IV usually have several choices to guide their approach to local resources. Firstly, firms can step into joint ventures with local firms; secondly, firms could employ more locally experienced personnel but still maintain their identity as a wholly owned foreign enterprise; and thirdly, firms could combine the first two options. Each choice has its pros and cons, and these will be illuminated in more detail with empirical cases in the subsequent chapters.

Notes

1. In 2020, 11.4% of South Africa's exports were to China, and 20.8% of its imports came from China, having increased to 45% and 18% (28%, 2016–2019), respectively, since 2016 (International Trade Centre, Trademap.org, accessed 29 June 2021).
2. Although they appear to be making a comeback under Xi Jinping.

3   Case Studies and 3D Institutional Model Analysis

This chapter will present ten case studies of South African firms which entered the Chinese market up until the core field-work in 2014, based on in-depth interviews with key stakeholders. This case study material has been supplemented by more recent follow-up investigations where these firms continue to operate in China. The case study firms are presented in five pairs, each representing class types of foreign-investing firms and business sectors in China. The aim is to identify the contextual factors which underpinned the study firms' successes and shortcomings as they first entered, then sought to consolidation their position within the Chinese market, set against the three-dimensional institutional (3D) model that was introduced in the previous chapter in order systematically to highlight how firms navigate institutional systems and negotiate with institutional actors in their international business development.

3.1 A Fine Line Between Success and Failure

The first pair of case studies compares two companies[1] from one of South Africa's strongest sectors, food and beverage, as they entered the potentially lucrative Chinese market. They adopted quite different business strategies, and this resulted in quite contrasting business outcomes.

Company A is one of the leading South African wineries based in Western Cape, and under the guidance of one of the most influential families in South Africa. Although it only commenced business at the turn of the present century, and was initially established with the UK market in mind, the company had expanded its business to 40 countries worldwide within a decade. In mid-2011 the company set up a joint venture (JV) with an overseas-Chinese company which specialises in direct sales in the retail industry, and within one year the company had shipped 2.9 million bottles of wine to China – a phenomenal achievement considering South Africa as a whole shipped only approximately 10 million bottles of wine to China in 2010/2011 (Western Cape Government, 2013).

DOI: 10.4324/9781003165668-3

My respondent informed me that to enter the Chinese market it was necessary for their business strategy to pass through several phases due to the complexity of contextual factors, such as language and a quite different wine-drinking culture. *Company A's* Chinese market expansion strategy relied significantly on the personal connections of its international marketing manager, who had almost 20 years of export experience in Asia. The marketing manager introduced one of his trusted Asian contacts, with whom he had cooperated for years, to the CEO and suggested that the CEO place this Asian contact on the company payroll. This was a ploy to nurture a relationship and expand networks, effectively establishing *guanxi*, because the Asian contact not only had vast experience of Asia but also held an influential position in the Northern Cape.

Initial progress was slow. The marketing manager recalls that 'The first year was hard and we did not do anything to develop the business apart from playing golf, drinking and socialising. For western companies this might be hard to accept but it is very necessary in China to build networks and trust with your potential partner!' One year later, just as the marketing manager had hoped and predicted, the business issues were formally put on the table and both companies started the first phase of their cooperation. *Company A* was introduced by their Asian contact to a joint venture (JV) partner (*Company A* owned 49% of the JV shares), an overseas Chinese company that was already established in the Chinese market with an extensive retail network, and its wine sales in China increased steadily. By mid-2011 the business was doing well, and started promoting new wine products to Chinese consumers.

Back in South Africa, *Company A* then embarked on a project to expand and deepen its business activities in China by nurturing prestige contacts and networks to take its Chinese presence to a higher level. The influential family behind *Company A* had a long-standing relationship and business connection with an ex-president of South Africa. This family connection later became one of the company's main assets in expanding its operation in the Chinese markets, allowing *Company A* to create a new product with his signature and presented as a limited edition 'signature wine' with only 5,000 bottles being released to the Chinese market. The first batch of 3,000 bottles sold out almost overnight, and the second release was also sold out even before the wine was bottled! This high-profile marketing strategy of using a famous figure – who was well known to the Chinese through previous state visits – to represent their product in China achieved fantastic results and also indirectly aided the promotion of their other products in the market. The limited-edition wine also had a French-sounding name and a chateau-style label which was perceived to be advantageous because Chinese consumers at the time considered French wines to be among the best in the world.

Analysis of Company A's *Chinese Business Strategies Within the 3D Institutional Model*

Figure 3.1 outlines the business scenarios and business transition strategies undertaken by *Company A*. The business initiative utilised a personal network (Cell I) and was then proactive in pursuing wider and higher-level network connections (Cell V). Whilst the relationship with high-profile contacts was nurtured by the company's privileged family background and connections, further business opportunities were also secured through other channels (Cell II). Later, in order to achieve a bigger margin from the Chinese market, they were (at the time the interview

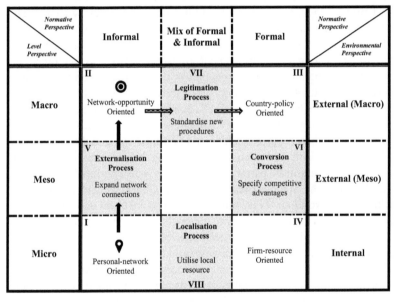

Key:

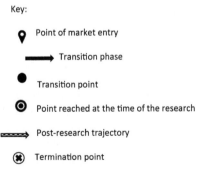

Q   Point of market entry

➤   Transition phase

●   Transition point

◎   Point reached at the time of the research

⇢   Post-research trajectory

✖   Termination point

Figure 3.1 Company A's Business Strategies Within the 3D Institutional Model

was conducted) hoping that the South African government would be able to finalise a better trade agreement with China on wine trade tariffs. *Company A* strategically engaged with government actors working on this initiative (Cell VII), although it has taken a while to achieve its objectives.[2]

The case of *Company A* shows that personal networks and the capacity for localisation born out of the previous experience of the newly appointed marketing manager were key to the firm's success in entering the Chinese market. Prior to this person's appointment the business strategy was in fact focused on the Western market and thus required adaptation and contextualisation. The marketing manager's Asian contact person enabled *Company A* to bridge the cultural and institutional divide between home and host market, laying a platform for future business success which, itself, was built on a nuanced understanding of the local contextual environment. Thus, an informal channel was opened up within the formal company structure to facilitate market entry and consolidation, which was reinforced via the firm's JV partner, which forms part of the externalisation process and network-opportunity mobilisation. This took time: 'friendship and trust come first before business [in China]'. Some JV partnerships are more successful than others: in the case of *Company A*, the fact that the CEOs of both partners visited each other in China and South Africa, and thereby formed a bond of friendship and mutual understanding, helped cement trust which is key to a successful JV partnership. *Company A* also nurtured a close relationship with the South African embassy in China, which helped further with local networking: 'every time we held a social event or business function, we always made sure to invite the "right" people [from the embassy]'.

There is little doubt that *Company A's* ability to draw on the patronage of an influential personality who was well known in China was also a significant factor in the firm's business success. But this, too, reflects how contextual awareness is crucial to the dynamics of operating in the Chinese market. The use of personalities in advertising is a strategy that has become increasingly prevalent in China (Hung *et al.*, 2011, 6), and one of the key ingredients of success in this regard is for the endorser to be credible, believable and authoritative (ibid., 7; Goldsmith *et al.*, 2000), which a former South African statesman most certainly is. The limited edition presidential signature brand was only available to the Chinese market: "We don't want to make too many, because we don't want to spoil or cheapen the label."

Company A provides a strong example of how a sensitivity to the local institutional environment, and most particularly the need to nurture relationships and networks, sometimes over a considerable period of time, can be crucial to business success in China, together with having the right product and an appropriate marketing strategy. A combination of these factors enabled the firm to pioneer a successful path into the Chinese market in a situation that was otherwise less than optimal: negotiations to establish a Free Trade Agreement between the PRC and South Africa, to rival those already in place for wine-exporting countries such as Chile, New Zealand and Australia, as well as Portugal via Macau, have been ongoing since 2010 but have yet to achieve concrete results.[3] 'The Chinese government has already reduced the duty payable on South African products by 50%, but South African products can still not compete with the prices of Chilean and New Zealand products. They pay almost 0% duty. The playing field is not level' complained the marketing manager. 'The South African government is not as active as the Chilean government when it comes to negotiating trade agreements'. In this sense, informal business processes have been used to compensate for limitations in formal institutional settings in delivering a company-specific advantage to *Company A*.

Company B is a restaurant chain which was also established in 2000 by two South African restaurateurs who both had sound and successful track records in the South African food and beverage industry. Their shared vision was to provide a quality dining experience to domestic and international customers. Within five years of opening their first restaurant in South Africa, they had managed to introduce their brand name to Australia, the Middle East, Israel and the UK with 12 successful restaurants altogether. The year 2009 saw the grand opening of their first outlet in Beijing, but after just 12 months the restaurant had to close down and they pulled out of China after making a loss of several million US dollars. This closure was almost incomprehensible given that they had received many top food awards and had been highly recommended by local media during the time they were operating. So what had happened to cause the closure of their first boutique restaurant in China?

The original plan had been to open a restaurant in Singapore as the company's first venture into Asia, but an opportunity in a newly completed retail project in Beijing appeared to provide a suitable location for their prestige brand, so they shifted their attention to China. The company's regional director for Asia Pacific, an internationally experienced businessman having previously worked in Australia, Singapore and the Middle East, was ambitious to capitalise on China's business potential, and was soon in negotiations with the retail project promoter, an American-Chinese businessman. Because of his previous business connections with the Middle East, the regional director decided to create a partnership with a large Middle Eastern retail group as the basis for entering the Chinese market, drawn by the significant financial support that the group offered. The China business was established as a Wholly-Owned Foreign Enterprise (WOFE), allowing the brand to control the business completely without any involvement from local businesses. This decision was the start of the many difficulties that *Company B* faced.

Establishing a WOFE (in Beijing) requires foreign investors to make a greater commitment compared to that of other business ventures such as a JV. The complicated procedures of initial company registration made the manager realise how difficult the Chinese institutional environment and requirements could be for first-time investors. From opening a bank account to employing staff, every step seemed to move at a snail's pace, with the inevitable frustrations which followed as a result of these delays. Not only did the manager have to deal with various government offices at metropolitan level, there were also those at district level and even some at smaller administrative levels. Language was another massive barrier for the new venture, 'Chinese are not willing to accept any other language than Mandarin to do business', the manager complained, 'and the only reliable people we found were Western companies operating in China – attorneys, accountants [because they could understand English]'. Because of these hurdles, setting up a new restaurant was extremely time-consuming. Months went by and they had still not opened their doors to customers.

When the time finally arrived to prepare the restaurant for opening, another wave of problems became apparent. Various inspections by lots of different local government departments had to be carried out before the work on the interior decorations could begin. The restaurant opening fell further behind schedule and the manager's patience was severely tested. Some of his local (Chinese) staff, concerned about the delays, suggested to him that he should be slightly more flexible in his approach to some of the more bureaucratic Chinese business practices in order to make things go more smoothly. The manager refused to follow their suggestions because he wanted to be in control and do things his own way. Eventually, after months of frustration, the restaurant finally opened and the company's focus shifted to deploying their tried-and-tested marketing approach to start promoting their products and service. Despite all this, the restaurant encountered further impediments: 'The project landlord just wasn't helpful in negotiating [a new lease contract] and didn't deliver what he agreed to deliver so we decided to close down!'; also, the Middle Eastern partner decided to withdraw from doing business in China – and after only a year the restaurant closed down at a loss of more than five million US dollars, and that was the end of *Company B's* China venture.

Even after the restaurant had closed down, the manager claimed he was still proud of what they had achieved:

> We did a very good job in making sure that we marketed ourselves to
> the Chinese community – when we started, our clientele was made up

of 90% foreigners and 10% Chinese. By the time we closed the restaurant we were already at 70% Chinese and 30% foreigners – we did a great job – we had the right media coverage and the right PR – we got the right people there, we got it right you know. We know even now that if we had stayed in China with the right relationship with the landlord of that [retail project] we would have made it work.

Analysis of Company B's *Chinese Business Strategies Within the 3D Institutional Model*

Company B's business life-span was rather short (Figure 3.2). The business started with the confidence that it would do well because of its premium service and brand reputation, as well as its successful business record in other countries (including some countries with difficult institutional environments) (Cell IV). However, the Chinese experience showed that, without a reliable local helping hand, the business was perhaps always going to struggle (Cell VIII). In sharp contrast to *Company A*, the new restaurant business relied very heavily on the firm's own resources to bridge the operational divide between home and host country. The underlying objective was to take the restaurant business to Asia, which probably meant that insufficient initial

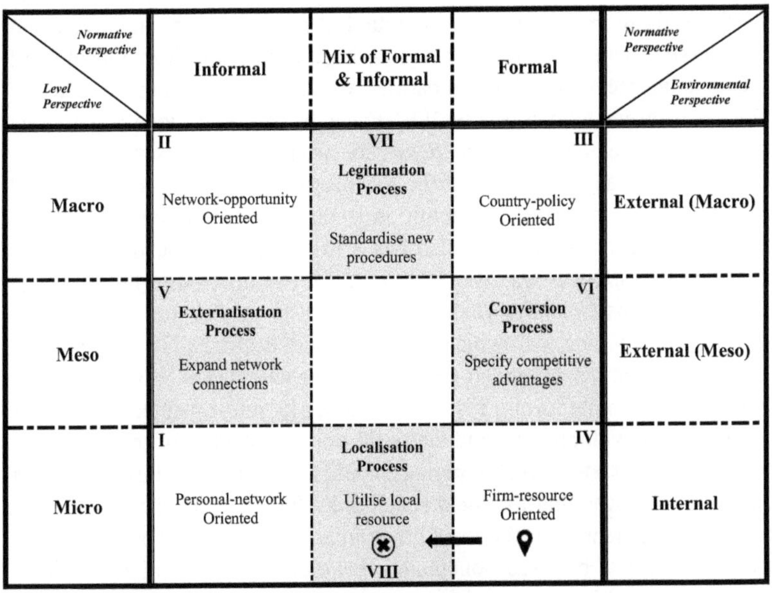

Normative Perspective / Level Perspective	Informal	Mix of Formal & Informal	Formal	Normative Perspective / Environmental Perspective
Macro	**II** Network-opportunity Oriented	**VII** Legitimation Process Standardise new procedures	**III** Country-policy Oriented	**External (Macro)**
Meso	**V** Externalisation Process Expand network connections		**VI** Conversion Process Specify competitive advantages	**External (Meso)**
Micro	**I** Personal-network Oriented	**Localisation Process** Utilise local resource ⊗ ← 📍 **VIII**	**IV** Firm-resource Oriented	**Internal**

Figure 3.2 Company B's Business Strategies Within the 3D Institutional Model

attention was given to locational specificities. The underlying, somewhat blasé philosophy seems to have been that success in other international markets (positive firm resource-oriented experience) would help determine success in China. As the market development manager explained 'we thought we had a proven model which worked in most countries that we had been to, we had tried different cultures!'

Whilst the business failure was partly blamed on an uncooperative project landlord, this may have been symptomatic of other shortcomings. Despite undeniably having a strong and quality product, efficient promotion and marketing mechanism, and wide implementation experience, insufficient attention was given to localisation processes. Their successful business experience in the Middle East had been built upon cooperation with a local partner which helped them build up their sales channels. Building on an apparently successful formula, the same partnership was behind the Beijing restaurant venture, and was the principal reason for following the WOFE model rather than looking for a JV with a local firm. Whilst *Company B* could thereby rely on its own resources – finance, product, marketing, etc. – it also meant that it had to deal alone with the institutional complexities of opening and operating a business in China. Staff engaged to navigate this contextual minefield, such as accountants and attorneys, were from trusted Western firms, even though there are many local professional companies available to help foreign enterprises set up a business in China, and this may even have been a further barrier to localisation. The manager admitted as much: 'we should have taken those lessons from the Middle East [entering a partnership with a local firm] to China, but the Middle Eastern partner was categorical that they wanted to do it on their own with us as a WOFE'. Once the partner decided to withdraw from the arrangement, *Company B* was not strong enough to survive.

Whilst it is easy to talk about the localisation of business strategies and the deployment of contextual intuition to navigate often complex institutional landscapes, serendipity also has a role to play in business success of failure. *Company A* was able to enjoy a fruitful relationship with a local partner, whereas *Company B* suffered through its association with the key stakeholder in China with which it had business dealings. He met the retail project manager, an American-Chinese lawyer who had achieved notoriety in Beijing by transforming historical landmarks into up-scale and luxury commercial developments, and was sold on the potential of the retail site. What he was not aware of, but perhaps could have found out through deeper due diligence, was that the local stakeholder had 'rented' the land for the retail development from the local government, based on his own networks and connections, but was nonetheless beholden to the local institutional environment, which restricted his own room for independent manoeuvre. Without local contacts and networks, and associated local intelligence,

Company B was powerless to influence the process when the restaurant's lease came up for renewal. The government stakeholders – the 'landlord' – had their own vision for the future which the local promoter was obliged to accept, and *Company B* simply lacked the right connections to negotiate for its own interests: "they [the local Chinese they knew] tried, but they were not powerful enough to make anything happen in China . . . you need to have the right level of connections and pay the right people to get things to happen on the ground." The manager of *Company B* complained of the 'hostile' business environment, which by international standards it may have appeared to be, but this betrays a very slim grasp of contextual realities in Beijing and elsewhere in China. The failure of the business was linked to its failure to move from the firm-resource oriented to personal-network oriented staged of the institutional model.

3.2 Financial Market: Different Targets, Different Strategies and Different Outcomes

The following four case studies are drawn from the financial sector: the first pair in insurance and the second pair in banking. The cases reveal differences in the firms' mind sets and business strategies which, in part, are attributable to differences in firm size, ownership structure, operation and management systems, as well as personal choices by key stakeholders.

Company C is a leading financial services institution in South Africa, having established their first office in the country in the early 1990s and become listed on the Johannesburg Stock Exchange (JSE) in 1999. One of the company's fully owned subsidiaries is the largest health insurance company in South Africa. Between 2000 and 2010, *Company C* set up JVs in the US and the UK with local partners in order to access Western markets. In August 2010, two years after initially establishing contact, *Company C* entered a joint venture arrangement with the then second largest Chinese insurance company, taking a 20% share of the new venture. Within the first year of operations the new company had 30,000 clients in the Chinese market.

Company C's core business approach centres on customer engagement and consumer well-being, delivering diverse products and services at competitive prices. Such business values enabled the company to gain a rapid foothold in the UK and US markets, but the Chinese market was more of a challenge. The business link-up happened opportunistically. They were initially approached by an international investment bank, which sought to mediate a potential connection with a Chinese health care company. *Company C* was at first somewhat disinterested as this was not their normal approach to entering a new market: 'Our approach when entering new markets was to go where we have good partners, as in the US and UK markets, otherwise there was no point! We did not have potential partners in China, and so we were not thinking of the Chinese market' explained one of the marketing directors. It was only once they had studied the figures from their intensive market research that they realised the Chinese markets held enormous potential for the kind of products and services they specialised in, and so they started to look seriously at business possibilities.

The Chinese company with which *Company C* later set up a joint venture was, like *Company C* itself, one of the biggest and longest-established firms in the Chinese insurance industry which also had a wholly owned health insurance subsidiary. It was seeking a foreign partner to set up a JV in order to improve its intellectual property (IP) on health insurance products and management. They had previously negotiated with several US and German companies, but little had been achieved due to the Chinese company's reluctance to cede 50% ownership of the JV. In 2009 the Chinese company was introduced to *Company C*, and the two firms came to an agreement whereby *Company C* would purchase shares in the Chinese company to form a business partnership. Although China's shifting policies on foreign insurance companies[4] slowed progress in their cooperation, the JV was eventually established following eight months of documentary procedures. At the time of the agreement, *Company C* was the only foreign health insurance company to own a 20% share of a joint venture in China.

Analysis of Company C's *Chinese Business Strategies Within the 3D Institutional Model*

Business opportunities can be initiated through high-level network connections, just as was the case with *Company C* when approached by an international investment bank seeking to broker a JV arrangement for the Chinese company (Cell II) (Figure 3.3). But to be able to take a business idea and convert it into an actual business deal, especially in China, requires a long legitimation process which involves a significant investment of time, finance and even emotion. As happened in this case, the Chinese policy environment can change almost overnight, and may appear to the outsider (and even the insider) to be almost arbitrary. In this instance, *Company C* experienced hurdles simply for being among the first insurance companies to seek a large shareholding in a JV with a Chinese firm. Nervous about the implications, the Chinese government quickly introduced a limit to equity shareholdings, placing institutionalised limits on the scale of *Company C's* involvement. Nonetheless, having successfully established a JV in this financial sector, *Company C* can be considered to have charted a path which has made it much easier for latecomers to follow (Cell VII). The conversion process (Cell VI) requires the firm to take a vital step from a position where they are 'comfortably' guided

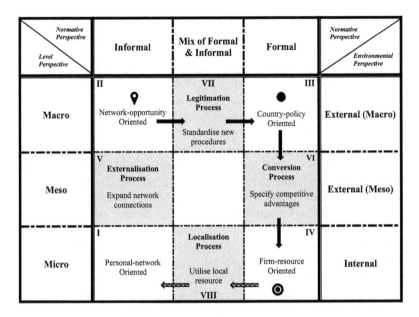

Figure 3.3 Company C's Business Strategies Within the 3D Institutional Model

and facilitated by the country's policy context (Cell III), to a situation where firms must work things out for themselves with a clear mind-set as to what products and services they can offer to the new market given its (in this case changing) policy framework, and what business strategies they must adopt in order to make the optimal utilisation of their firm's resources and competitive advantage (Cell IV). Also, forming a JV partner with a local Chinese company, *Company C* had to learn quickly how engage effectively with the local partner in order to exploit the fullest potential of the local market (Cell VIII), which required a lot of patience, flexibility and understanding.

Whilst *Company C* largely relied on its own resources and resourcefulness to enter the Chinese market, certain external influences were also key to a successful process. As we discussed in the previous section, serendipity can often play a role. The Chinese company – one of the earliest insurers in the Chinese market – happened to be looking for a foreign partner to help improve its IP, and had been assisted in this process through its formal and informal business connections since the 1990s with, *inter alia*, the China Banking and Insurance and Regulatory Commission (CBIRC) and the Bank of China (BOC). *Company C* responded to this network-oriented opportunity rather than initiated it, but the partner firm's high-level institutional connections allowed it to make a relatively smooth transition into the Chinese market. Compared to other sectors, insurance was, and still is, a tightly controlled and regulated industry in China, but at the time of the cementation of the JV the Chinese regulators were inexperienced at processing such a transaction. Thus, *Company C* was faced with the need to navigate a mutable institutional (i.e. regulatory) environment. This turned out to be a double-edged sword for *Company C*: on the one hand, as one of the first insurance companies to establish a JV in China, it could establish the standards and procedures for this kind of transaction (Cell VII), thereby setting a benchmark for later firms to follow; but on the other hand, *Company C* had to face the risks and costs associated with a lack of established regulations and standardised legal procedures. *Company C's* managers who were involved in the transaction nonetheless found that the institutional environment, although frustrating at times, was flexible enough to allow progress towards completion of the JV arrangement, in part because of the local partner's connections with the regulator. As one manager said, "it's a question of experience. The more CIRC deal with this type of thing the more efficient their systems and processes will become. And the stronger and more robust your (Chinese) regulators are, actually the better it will be for their own industries in the long term." *Company C* had little wriggle room in terms of complying with the prevailing institutional situation (Cell III) because its JV partner was a listed shareholding company with responsibilities to its shareholders, some of which were state-owned entities. Its 20 years of growth and operational experience in South Africa and other African markets helped prepare *Company C* to adapt to the imperfect institutional environment it encountered in China.

Another company-specific competitive advantage that helped in the conversion process (Cell VI) was their advanced health insurance IP, which was something the local JV partner was keen to acquire and which put *Company C* in a strong position in terms of the leverage it bestowed the Chinese company in steering a path through the country's bureaucratic systems. As the *Company C* manager stated: "We looked to the Chinese partner for some real insight into the Chinese market, which they, as a Chinese company, have a much better understanding of than we do. . . . We bring the expertise and experience in health insurance products and services, while they bring their local knowledge and insights to tell us what is proper for the market. It is absolutely essential that you don't go into a market that you don't fully understand."

Since the JV was established, Chinese consumers' interest in health and well-being has grown exponentially, significantly justifying *Company C's* investment in China and negotiating the bureaucratic hurdles that this entailed. As *Company C* considers a deeper involvement in the Chinese market, the assistance of the Chinese partner in the localisation process (Cell VIII) will be particularly important given the considerable diversity of the Chinese health care sector, determining that a uniform approach to expansion is unlikely to succeed. At the time of the research, however, *Company C* was in no rush to explore wider opportunities within China, preferring instead a gradual incremental approach which allows it personnel (foreign and local) to accumulate knowledge and experience before expanding its Chinese business.

Although **Company D** also operates in the insurance industry, its experience in China was quite different to that of *Company C*. Established in 1980,[5] *Company D* is the largest privately owned insurance company in South Africa, employing 2,300 people worldwide and providing a wide range of insurance products to more than 6.5 million domestic and international policy-holders. Although *Company D* has a presence in the UK and US markets, its focus is on developing country markets where its African roots and experience provide a competitive advantage. In 2006, an Australian-Chinese individual who worked for *Company D's* Australian subsidiary contacted the South African headquarters about a business opportunity in China, where the insurance market was relatively underdeveloped but with huge potential. Having recently opened an office in India, which was also a challenging market for foreign business to penetrate, head office was open-minded about exploring possibilities in China, and so a market development manager was sent to China in late 2006 to lay the groundwork for a new business. In mid-2007 *Company D* set up a Representative Office in Beijing for their insurance and brokerage business, which gave the company a presence in China but only initially as a non-profit entity. Three years later they paired with a local retail franchise chain company to establish a joint ventured consultation business for retail insurance products in the Chinese market. From 2012 they started a full insurance and brokerage business as a WOFE after satisfying the 'five-year rep office' requirement as stipulated by CIRC and other China financial regulators.[6]

From the start of its involvement in the insurance industry, *Company D* had built a network of relationships with business partners from various industries, and this convinced them that sound partnerships were a vital part of a successful business development strategy. Thus, during the period as a Representative Office in China, *Company D* searched for and then initiated cooperation with local business partners. Whilst *Company D* possesses a license to see insurance products in South Africa, their approach to the Chinese market was different: 'We are not there to compete with the mainland Chinese insurance companies, for us it is all about bringing innovative products and innovative distribution ideas to the Chinese market in partnership with a local insurance company', according to a director of the company's international division. This business perspective was reflected in the way they selected business partners. Two years after their arrival in China the partner they chose to cooperate with was a comparatively small local retailer, and then three years later, in 2012, they secured a contract with a large national insurance company to promote new products. Their market intelligence had told them that markets like that in China required patience and time to nurture relationships and to allow local customers to become familiar with their insurance products and services. Thus the 'bedding in' period whilst operating as a Representative Office was advantageous to *Company D* in allowing these relationships gradually to mature, whilst its private ownership model also allowed it to focus on long-term rather than short-term economic gains, which would not have been possible as a listed company answerable to shareholders.

Analysis of Company D's *Chinese Business Strategies Under the 3D Institutional Model*

As these paired case studies show, companies in the same industry do not necessarily adopt an identical business approach in penetrating and operating within the Chinese market (Figure 3.4). Each has its own internal firm-level institutional arrangements to engage those that they encounter in foreign market. The 'opening gambit' often determines the path towards eventual business development, and this may be influenced as much by the 'personality' of the

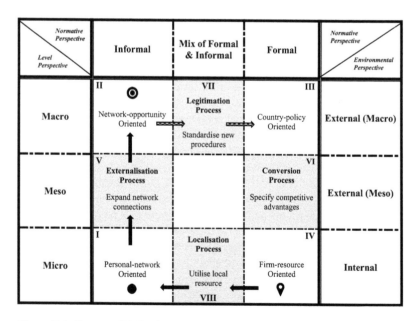

Figure 3.4 Company D's Business Strategies Within the 3D Institutional Model

firm as by the economic rationale of its business venture. Compared with *Company C, Company D* was constrained by the size of the firm, which would ordinarily have made it less competitive in the Chinese market. However, by virtue of a personal recommendation (Cell I), they identified a niche market where they could gain a foothold in China and also time to allow the deepening of their business contacts (Cell V). A long-vision business development strategy enabled them to nurture higher-level business cooperation opportunities both inside and outside China (Cell II), and thereby consolidate their business legitimation (Cell VII).

A key ingredient in *Company D's* successful entry into the Chinese market was its prior experience of operating in developing countries (Cell IV). Once the prospect of expanding the business to China arose, *Company D* started the internal search for a business development manager (firm-centred resource) to lead this initiative. Initially there were few volunteers, but one manager who had just returned to South Africa from setting up a branch office in India offered his services. His overseas experience was invaluable, and he quickly set about building a 'China team' from within the company to identify the human and material resources required to start operations in China. They managed to recruit onto the team the Chinese-Australian manager who had originally suggested the idea to *Company D*, and who was able to help overcome language barriers as well as familiarising *Company D* with the rules and regulations governing foreign financial enterprises investing in China. This manager also convinced the company's HQ of the need to 'go local' (localisation), which also necessitated awareness of the cultural context within which they would be operating. To help with this process, they employed the services of the Beijing Foreign Enterprise Human Resources Service Co. (FESCO)[7] to assist them with the establishment of their first Representative Office. They also began the search for a local Chinese candidate for the role of China operations manager. In early 2010 *Company D* found a new manager, a person of Chinese origin who had lived and studied in South Africa, to operate their Chinese business in place of a South African manager. At the same time, *Company D* joined forces with a local retail company to establish a JV to distribute new retail insurance products to the Chinese market. They used local knowledge and the manager's personal networks to overcome the hurdle of not being allowed under Chinese law to sell insurance products without possessing the appropriate license by registering as a consultancy business, with the associated license, and retailing their products as consultation services, and the law allows.

Consolidation and expansion of their China business relied heavily on three key managers and the relationships they nurtured with key stakeholders (externalisation). The first South African manager was active in developing a network of contacts, both in the South African Embassy and among the local Chinese business community, in order to get the business established on the ground. The Chinese second manager used her local knowlédge to expand connections with wider business networks. The International Division manager based in the South African headquarters focused on building relations with higher-level institutions in the international sphere (network opportunity), most particularly projects associated with the BRICS countries. Through these, in 2012 *Company D* was able to secure a contract with a large Chinese state-owned investment company, the then-largest insurance company outside the life insurance sub-sector. This was the fruit of their endeavours during their five years as a Representative Office: whilst not profitable from a business point of view, this period of 'testing the water' was invaluable for *Company D* in overcoming the many challenges associated with entering the Chinese market.

In 2014, *Company D* built upon its experience of operating in China by establishing a China Desk back at HQ in South Africa, designed to identify further opportunities for developing business links with China, and for connecting with overseas Chinese companies operating in Africa. In 2019, China further relaxed the entry requirements for foreign-funded enterprises in the insurance industry, allowing foreign personal insurance institutions to invest directly in the establishment of insurance companies in China. This allows foreign insurance companies a more level playing field with their Chinese competitors. In 2019, the premium income of foreign insurance companies increased by 29.9% year-on-year, surpassing the 12.2% growth rate of Chinese insurance companies (Deloitte, 2020).

Moving on to the second pair of company case studies in the financial sector, in comparison with South African insurance companies' business cooperation with Chinese partners, **South African banks** are involved in much larger-volume capital transactions, and this is reflected in the more conservative business strategies that they adopted.

Company E is the largest bank by assets in Africa, and has a more than 150-year banking business history in South Africa. From the 1990s it started expanding its business into other parts of Africa and some other emerging markets, including Asia. Today they employ some 54,000 people and operate in more than 30 countries, most of which are emerging country markets. With regard to *Company E's* foothold in Asia, in the early 1990s it established a Representative Office in Hong Kong, and another in Shanghai in the late 1990s, both in support of South African business clients with interests in Asia. In early 2000 the company established a resource-focused business in China, a WOFE advisory venture, to facilitate its business with commodity trading and cross-border mergers and acquisitions (M&A). Such China-centred activities were relatively limited in scope, focusing principally on *Company E's* African business clients. At this stage they found it hard to compete with the large Chinese banks and those from the US and Europe. They needed to find a niche market in order to become established in China.

In 2007 *Company E* announced a multi-billion dollar strategic business partnership with the largest Chinese commercial bank, *Chinese Bank X*. During the first five years of the collaboration, *Company E* established a Representative Office for the banking business, and a further two WOFE ventures as consultation businesses, one of which supports South African corporate customers in their international investment business and trade activities, whilst the other mainly serves Chinese state-owned company clients to help facilitate their international investments outside China.

Despite its status as Africa's oldest commodity bank, *Company E* was in fact constrained by its size in entering the Chinese market: whilst *Chinese Bank X* was ranked in the world's top five banks by asset size (*The Banker's Top 1000 World Banks 2012 Rankings*), *Company E* was ranked outside the top 100. But to compensate, *Company E* was able to use to its advantage its rich international business experience, and its advanced technical and information support systems for dealing with mining and other resource companies (firm resource), both of which the Chinese banking counterpart lacked.

The two companies' executives initiated the business cooperation when they first met in Beijing in 2005. Over the following two years the two companies kept in regular communication about their prospective business collaboration, and formal business negotiations commenced in Autumn 2007. It took just 45 days for the two sides to reach agreement on the basis for cooperation, which surprised many business commentators, including the local South African mass media. The two companies formed a 'strategic alliance' which involved *Chinese Bank X* purchasing a 20% stake in *Company E*, which in turn agreed to facilitate the Chinese bank's business dealings in overseas markets, particularly in emerging markets. The transaction was formalised within five months, and was the biggest financial acquisition deal in South Africa up to that point in time. Five years later, the strategic alliance appeared to have been a business win-win for both sides: through the deal, *Company E* received a large capital injection, especially in hard currency, to sustain its asset growth and physical expansion; meanwhile, *Chinese Bank X* has, with the assistance of *Company E*, been able to expand its operations into emerging markets in Africa and Latin America, thereby expanding its foreign business investment profile.

Analysis of Company E's *Chinese Business Strategies Under the 3D Institutional Model*

Company E had aspired to becoming established in the Chinese market for at least ten years before they linked up with *Chinese Bank X* (Figure 3.5). Upon

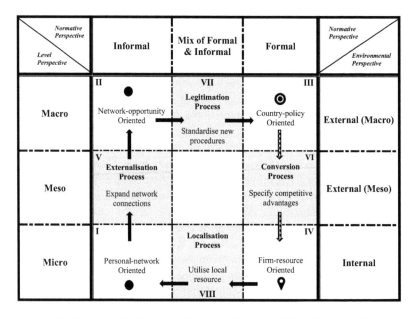

Figure 3.5 Company E's Business Strategies Within the 3D Institutional Model

entering China as a Representative Office, *Company E* relied largely on its own business resources (Cell IV), which initially constrained its business scope (Cell I). Faced with language and cultural hurdles, *Company E* started to employ local Chinese as well as native South Africans with appropriate language skills and local knowledge (Cell V). Nonetheless, the nature of the business services and products offered by *Company E* meant that it became associated with quite high-profile institutions in China, most of which were large Chinese state-owned enterprises (SOEs) (Cell II). As a result of these connections, *Company E* was able to build a solid platform for later even higher-profile business development. The multi-billion-dollar deal was a high-level institutional arrangement (Cell II), and was expedited very quickly because of the connections that had been built up during the prior two-year period, but also because both parties were able to work together most efficiently (Cell VII). *Company E* recognised that, by working with a large Chinese SOE, it would be strictly beholden to state financial sector policies and regulations (Cell III), and this underpinned its rather conservative approach when compared with its dealings, in collaboration with *Chinese Bank X*, with markets outside China. At the same time, its collaboration with an influential Chinese SOE allowed *Company E* to take advantage of its Chinese partner's capacity also to influence state policy (Cell VI).

The establishment of Representative Offices in Hong Kong and then Shanghai in the 1990s, and later the two WOFEs, enabled *Company E* to build an albeit marginal local presence in the Chinese banking sector (localisation). These allowed the company to start building networks with local Chinese resource and commodity companies. They also employed local staff and Mandarin-speaking South Africans to help with the localisation process. Although its degree of localisation during its early period in China was relatively limited, it allowed *Company E* to establish a platform – in terms of personnel, business capacity and networks – that would prove to be invaluable in its later business development. *Company E* also had a high-level business director based in China who nurtured and maintained high-profile connections with business associates and customers, particularly among indigenous state-owned companies. This director met his to-be counterpart at an international financial industry conference in Beijing in 2005, and this turned out to be the prelude to a very fruitful business relationship (externalisation).

For both companies this business opportunity seemed to arrive at the right time (opportunity oriented). During the initial period of negotiations, the global financial recession hit the banking sector, and left *Company E* in need of an injection of financial capital. The Chinese bank, meanwhile, was looking to modernise and internationalise its operations. Both parties initially explored collaborative possibilities with other companies,[8] but none could meet the expectations of the respective banks' shareholders to the same extent as the eventual 'strategic alliance' between *Company E* and *Chinese Bank X*. An important factor in this regard was the size of the stake in *Company E* that was taken by the Chinese bank, 20%. This was enough to give *Chinese Bank X* a position on *Company E's* board, but was not so large as to threaten the interests of existing shareholders. The deal was also expedited very quickly because the 'top people' in both companies were in regular and direct communication with each other. The Chinese firm, for its part, established an intensive study group consisting of 30 members from ten departments to conduct a pre-feasibility study. This 'due diligence' provided a large volume of supporting materials which helped in the latter application for government institutional approvals (legitimation). The banking and other regulators in both South Africa and China attached great significance to this transaction because of its considerable economic and political importance to both countries (Mboweni, 2004). It took just five months to obtain the formal approval of the South African Reserve Bank and the China Banking Regulatory Commission.

Chinese Bank X's engagement with Africa after the establishment of the strategic alliance was rapid, encouraged strongly by China's 'go global' policy to invest and acquire quality assets in international (and especially emerging) markets. *Company E* already has a lot of experience operating in these markets, with advanced technological and information systems, and was thus eminently capable of facilitating *Chinese Bank X's* transactions through their established institutional networks and customer resources. In return for its involvement, *Company E* received an injection of capital from each successful deal, which in turn facilitated its organic growth and expansion into other markets, including China. In contrast, *Company E* adopted a more gradualist approach towards the Chinese market. Because of the involvement of Chinese SOE shareholders, *Company E* was aware that this would require rigid compliance with government policies, and was concerned that this might constrain its business operations in China. This was nonetheless traded off against the access *Chinese Bank X* facilitated to wider consumer markets within China (conversion process).[9] Although *Chinese Bank X's* existing customers would not be converted directly into *Company E's* customer base, its enormous customer foundation provided a platform for *Company E* to practice new business initiatives.

Both companies exchanged employees to enhance understanding and learning from each other. Just after the establishment of the strategic partnership with *Chinese Bank X*, *Company E* set up another WOFE business venture in Beijing in 2009 in order to strengthen its presence in the Chinese markets, and at the same time shorten both the physical and psychological distance from their major Chinese SOE client and various levels of government for the purpose of maintaining and expanding their business networks. One manager from *Company E* who used to be based in China said, "doing business in China is all about *guanxi* (networks and connections), and it is policy oriented. But if policy-related issues arise during our business, we'll go to our partner to get them to solve the problem."

Company F is one of the top three largest banks by market capitalisation listed on the Johannesburg Stock Exchange (JSE). Its retail banking history dates back to the mid-Nineteenth Century. Three entrepreneurs started an investment banking business for the company in the late 1970s, and it was listed on the JSE in 1998. Through major subsidiary financial divisions, *Company F* provides services to 9 million customers worldwide and has expanded its business to the rest of the African continent, as well as to Europe, the Middle East and Asia, employing 45,000 people world-wide. In 2007 *Company F* established a Representative Office in Shanghai, and two years later signed a 'strategic co-operation' agreement with *Chinese Bank Y* to co-operate on various Sino-African projects. *Company F* has a strong entrepreneurial culture and holds to a business vision to build long-term franchise value and generate sustainable returns for its shareholders, so hitherto its principal focus has been on Africa. But with the growing strength of emerging economies like China, and their increasing interest in Africa, the bank realised that it would be foolish to overlook the opportunities this could bring to their business in South Africa.

Similar to *Company E* just described, *Company F* adopted a fairly conservative approach towards China and the Chinese market, in line with the company's general global strategy. Indeed, *Company F* was the business that *Chinese Bank X* initially discussed a partnership with in 2007 before the idea was rejected by *Company F's* shareholders, prompting it to turn to *Company E*. Two years later, however, *Company F* was back in the game, establishing a 'strategic co-operation' agreement with *Chinese Bank Y*. This was in part driven by the increasing numbers of Chinese companies expanding into South Africa and Africa as a whole, including many large infrastructure and resource extraction projects, and *Company F* saw the business value of becoming involved, in the process potentially expanding its physical presence in other African countries. Whilst on the surface it may appear that *Company F* was seeking to 'catch up' with its competitor, *Company E*, its approach to engaging the Chinese market was quite different, based largely on a Memorandum of Understanding (MoU) rather than a full legal agreement.

Analysis of Company F's *Chinese Business Strategies Under the 3D Institutional Model*

Company F entered China with the clear intention of serving the interests of its clients in the overseas markets, which was a successful business model that *Company F* had used in other markets (particularly the Middle East) before China (Cell IV) (Figure 3.6). The company's clients were becoming more active in trade and investment in China, and *Company F's* expansion into this market was originally intended as a means of supporting its clients' Chinese business activities by providing the requisite financial services (firm resources). One manager from *Company F* said: "we support South African firms in China: their projects in China might not be convincible to the Chinese banks in order to secure loans, but we know them and trust their HQ in South Africa, so we can help these firms." As a result, *Company F's* China journey was 'pushed' by its existing customers' needs.

Company F was less ambitious in terms of the Chinese market itself, and wanted to test the water before going too far. It considered itself to be insufficiently competitive compared to both domestic Chinese banks and other large foreign banks because their brand was not yet well known in China. They were nonetheless conscious that to have a local partner would make things easier (localisation). This partner, *Chinese Bank Y*, was one of the 'big four' Chinese state-owned banks, and was one of the earliest Chinese banks to have a presence in South Africa. Like *Company F*, it also specialised in business investment. *Company F* was fortunate in having a South African manager with a Chinese background who was able to help liaise with *Chinese Bank Y* to build the basis for cooperation (Cell VIII to Cell I). Although

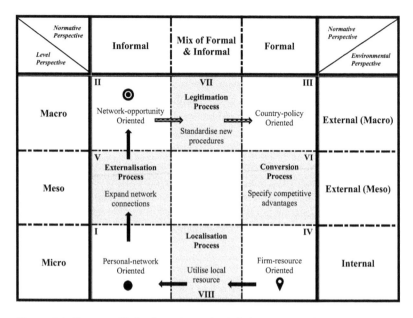

Figure 3.6 Company F's Business Strategies Within the 3D Institutional Model

this cooperation did not extend further than a MoU, the Chinese bank was helpful and proactive in facilitating connections with higher-level institutional networks, via their own clients in the Chinese market, as well as via participating international institutional initiatives such as BRICS (Cell V). Later still, *Company F* was selected by a Chinese state-funded organisation to act as regional partner to generate and enhance business opportunities for both countries (Cell II). To become feasible, this arrangement required a formal legislation process (Cell VII).

Company F adopted an incremental approach to its engagement with the Chinese market, initially supporting its existing clients' Chinese ventures, but in the process building brand awareness for *Company F's* products and services, whilst also using *Chinese Bank Y's* brand name to attract new customers and business opportunities in China. Thus, as in the case of *Company E*, the five-year operation of a Representative Office in China, whilst of limited utility for short-term financial rewards, was invaluable in terms of establishing the brand in China and laying the foundations for later business development. *Company F* was recently chosen as a cooperation partner by one of China's government-funded financial organisations collectively to promote Sino-African business trade and investment projects. *Company F* has also been actively involved in the BRICS' plan to form a regional development bank, which will create unprecedented business opportunities for

Company F to expand their business range and presence in these dynamic emerging markets.

3.3 Machinery Market: Business Partners Control the Fate of the Business

The machinery industry is a sector where South African firms are in a strong position to take advantage of opportunities in China because of their advanced technologies and management skills. The down side is that they face weak protection from Chinese institutions, not least in the safeguarding of intellectual property (IP). *Companies G and H* are two South African machinery manufacturers whose experience in China followed two quite different trajectories based on contrasting approaches to navigating the country's institutional environment.

Company G is a machinery distribution group for many large international heavy industry brands, having more than 100 years of involvement in this sector and now consisting of a wide range of business divisions. It operates in 27 countries worldwide and employs more than 19,000 people, of whom 35% are located outside South Africa. In 2008 *Company G* started to give serious consideration to entering China because of the growing number of Chinese contracting companies coming to Africa to purchase their products. Having a presence in China would put them in a strong position to capitalise on the rapidly rising demand for heavy machinery. *Company G* also looked to become a conduit for cheaper machinery from China which could be in demand in several African countries. By 2011 the company had established WOFE ventures in both mainland China and Hong Kong.

Although *Company G* had had a limited involvement in China before 2008, drawn by the country's equipment needs for industrial development and infrastructure construction, finding an appropriate person to manage the company's affairs in China was the key factor in launching a full-scale market entry in 2011. The appointed market development manager was an ethnic Chinese who was born outside mainland China and had migrated to South Africa at a young age in the early 1990s. His cultural ability to straddle the continents of Africa and Asia offered a competitive advantage that is not often enjoyed by South African firms operating in the Asian markets.

Analysis of Company G's *Chinese Business Strategies Under the 3D Institutional Model*

As one of the few South African firms to establish a Wholly-Owned Foreign Enterprise in the machinery and construction industry in China, *Company G's* business strategy was quite distinctive compared with the JV

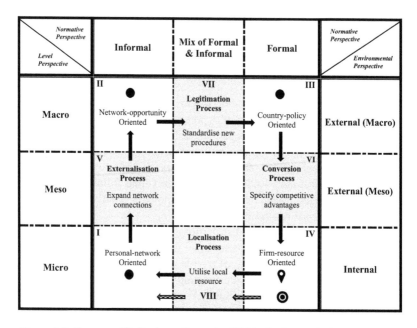

Figure 3.7 Company G's Business Strategies Within the 3D Institutional Model

model (Figure 3.7). The company's strategy in relation to the 3D Institutional Model can be demonstrated thus: the company decided to have a presence in the Chinese market because their contracting Chinese client pool was rapidly expanding, so they needed a Chinese base for their operations (Cell IV). *Company G* already had extensive experience of operating in developing markets, but their Mandarin-speaking, ethnic Chinese business manager was key to walking them through the Chinese 'internalisation' process (Cell VIII). This person was instrumental in enabling *Company G* build up networks with local businesses, and the time-consuming process of setting up a WOFE allowed many opportunities for *Company G* to solidify its business relationship with clients in an informal manner. The business development manager also eased the company's path through the higher-level institutional environment which both smoothed progress with market entry and consolidation, and also opened up wider and bigger business opportunities (Cell 1). Through this process, *Company G* was able to reach certain 'VIP' contacts within the upper-level institutions (Cell II) who were able to put the company in touch with key actors in the Chinese SOEs with which they were involved, although, inevitably, forming connections with SOE actors constrained the flexibility of *Company G's* business practices because of the need to follow all laws and policies to the letter (Cell V). The ethnic Chinese business development manager was nonetheless well-versed in navigating the policy environment in such a way as to minimise *Company G's* exposure to risk (Cell III). These high-level connections were advantageous to *Company G* when new Chinese preferential policies were introduced for Sino-African business co-operation, setting in motion a new business cycle which built upon the foundations established during *Company G's* initial foray into the Chinese market.

Finding the right people to lead a business venture in a vastly different cultural and institutional context is – as we have seen in previous case studies – often crucial to business success and most particularly the localisation process. The to-be business development manager, in his mid-20s, only joined *Company G* a few months before the company decided to start its business venture in China. Although there were doubts within the company about the manager's capability to take on such an important role, the general consensus was that his cultural background and experience, and the fact that his family business had frequent dealings with China, meant that he had the right credentials to facilitate the firm's localisation in mainland China. The fact that he was already a loyal employee of *Company G* also obviated the need to identify a local partner in China, with the incumbent risks this potentially presented.

As anticipated, it was not long before the new market development manager began to realise that being able to speak Mandarin and understand Chinese culture was in itself insufficient to start a new business in China. Networking with individuals, businesses and organisations would be key to business success. As the manager reflected on his first visit to China in 2008: "In some ways it did surprise me. I had previously only talked to Chinese customers on the phone before and I thought that Chinese people would be very traditional and conservative, but when I came here I realised I was more traditional than they were . . ." With regard to *guanxi* or personal connections affecting business, he commented: "there are far fewer principles in the way of doing things! It initially feels like in China you probably can't do anything because of all the constraints, but in reality you can do everything and anything if you are capable enough. If you are successful in building up relationships for the business, you will often be able to access the 'VIP channel'!"

Using personal networks in China can, however, sometimes prove to be a double-edged sword. *Company G* nurtured good relations with high-level SOE officials, but membership of *guanxi* networks brings costs as well as benefits. In exchange to opening various windows of opportunity for *Company G* and facilitating its localisation process, the high-level officials were sometimes looking for 'commissions' when their SOEs placed lucrative orders for *Company G's* heavy construction equipment. Following China's own rules and regulations, and *Company G's* international trading principles, would mean that no such 'additional payments' would be allowable, but this would also risk losing some multi-million-dollar contracts. To circumvent this dilemma, the business development manager of *Company G* sought a middle path which would seal the deal without compromising the company's ethical principles. This was achieved by finding a third-party company, which was a reliable network member of both *Company G* and the SOE, to mediate the deal. *Company G* would sell the machinery to the third-party company at a discount on the standard price, and the SOE would buy the same products from the third-party company by paying the standard price, but at the same time would receive a separate commission as a 'discount', whilst the third-party company would also gain a percentage of the difference between the sale price and the standard price for mediating business deal. All parties would be satisfied with this arrangement: *Company G* secured a deal and maintained a valuable relationship with the client and the client's immediate connections and networks, whilst the client received the products at an acceptable price together with certain commissions, as did the mediating company, together with networking opportunities with two big clients. Whilst such an arrangement was morally problematic, such arrangements were commonplace and the business opportunity – and also good connections with influential clients – would have been lost without this flexible response. But to be able to build such an arrangement first necessitated the building of trust between the various parties, and required a nuanced understanding of local contextual processes and an ability to 'read the signs' as negotiations unfolded. Networks are key to doing business in China.

Whilst *Company G's* market development manager was clearly versed in the informal institutional 'rules of the game', navigating the formal institutional environment in the process of business licence registration (legitimation) was a somewhat complex process. *Company G* originally proposed to set up a WOFE to cover the business scope of import, export and machinery distribution projects in China, as well as a logistics consultancy. The proposed WOFE would involve eight discrete dealerships, with *Company G* being the major shareholder. Such a business arrangement would have been quite complex for *Company G* to manage, and it would have been complicated and time-consuming to arrange all the necessary business licences. Based on his Chinese background and prior business experience, the development manager devised an alternative business structure which took full advantage of the Chinese institutional context (i.e. what was allowable within the Chinese legal and policy framework): the company would register as two business entities, one in mainland China and one in the Hong Kong Special Administrative Region (SAR). The rationale behind this move was that the taxation system and foreign capital controls in Hong Kong were much more favourable to foreign investors compared with mainland China. In the process, the South African HQ could use the Hong Kong business account as a firewall to protect their major business: 'If there is something wrong here [in China or Hong Kong], we have a firewall to cushion us, because Hong Kong is a place with only limited liabilities. Such a 'limited liability' would not affect our UK or South African business operations. At the end of the day we are listed on the JSE and LSE, and these are our core businesses and main body, so we have to protect them'. On the other hand, *Company G* could then use the Hong Kong entity to re-invest in the mainland Chinese markets to set up branch offices, and the business scope would be much wider and less restricted by the formal business registration rules and regulations in mainland China. Through this scheme, *Company G* was able quickly and straightforwardly to acquire the required business licenses before they formally commenced operations in China.

Having successfully negotiated the Chinese formal institutional environment (country-policy oriented) to establish, licence and operate its Chinese subsidiary, the platform was laid to expand the business further (business transforming process), at which stage informal institutional practices returned to the fore. By the time the business was formally in operation in 2011, *Company G's* relationship with its various Chinese business clients and contacts, which it had been fostering since 2008, had matured sufficiently to allow both sets of parties to negotiate the terms of more substantial business co-operation arrangements. *Company G* looked to take advantage of Chinese state policies giving preferential treatment to deals involving investment from China to Africa. Having established a formal business presence in China and built a good track record of dealing with influential Chinese SOE clients, *Company G* had a competitive advantage in bidding for projects in Africa that involved large Chinese SOEs, including those with which *Company G* had previously co-operated. True to form, not long after their establishment in Shanghai, *Company G* successfully bid for a multi-million-dollar project to supply all the machinery for a mining project in a southern African country, the principal investor in which was a large Chinese SOE from South China.

Company H has been heavily involved with large infrastructure projects inside China since the mid-1990s, when China's economic boom led to a massive increase in infrastructure building. *Company H* is a high-tech-oriented equipment company with a prime focus on the development and application of proprietary technology in ground improvement and preparation. The company has a number of international patents for their advanced impact compaction technology. Although it is a comparatively small private company within the construction industry, *Company H's* competitive advantage derives from its heavy investment of time and capital in the development and refinement of new technologies for infrastructure construction, leading to the company's business expansion from South Africa to the rest of the African continent, Europe, America and Australia, and more recently Hong Kong and mainland China.

Company H started its business journey in China in 1995 when it was contracted to a large airport project in Hong Kong. The success of the Hong Kong project as well as the appealing market opportunities emerging from mainland China convinced *Company H* that there would be a strong future demand for their advanced technology coupled with their international business experience. As with several of the case studies discussed previously, *Company H's* business consolidation in China relied heavily on a local Chinese contact and business partner who was originally from north China but had lived in South Africa for many years. *Company H* established a WOFE and became involved in more than 200 projects spread across 25 provinces in China. However, its undoubted business success was marred by bitter legal struggles between *Company H* and several local companies over intellectual property rights (IPR) infringements. Although *Company H* eventually won these legal cases, they were costly and time-consuming, and this, together with what appeared to *Company H* to be a 'non-rational' Chinese institutional environment, led to the company's eventual withdrawal from the Chinese markets.

Analysis of Company H's *Chinese Business Strategies Under the 3D Institutional Model*

Company H entered the mainland Chinese market after its successful business venture in Hong Kong (Figure 3.8). In order to protect their IP, which formed the company's key competitive advantage, they elected to set up a WOFE rather than enter into a JV with a Chinese partner, and also relied on their own personnel to manage the development of their Chinese enterprise (Cell IV). They were nonetheless open to co-operating on a contractual basis with local partners, facilitated through local contacts, in order to compensate for their 'newness' in the market, but in strict compliance with company protocols that they have applied in their business dealings around the world (Cell VIII). However, as their business grew, *Company H* almost inevitably experienced serious trouble with their Chinese partners over IP infringements. What *Company H* found particularly difficult was that many of their clients were large state-owned enterprises which usually occupied higher-level institutional positions and with high-level connections, but these enterprises and their personnel lacked fundamental knowledge about IP rights and protection. Compared with many other foreign firms who invested their efforts in both formal and informal networking with higher-level institutions and local stakeholder as they sought new business opportunities, *Company H* channelled most of their efforts into protecting their own IP at all institutional levels (Cell V, Cell II). In

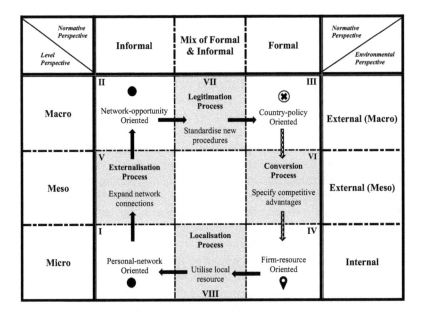

Figure 3.8 Company H's Business Strategies Within the 3D Institutional Model

the end, after a decade of painful and frustrating legal proceedings, *Company H* was finally successful in establishing that its Chinese partners had infringed their IP (Cell VII), but by this time *Company H* was completely drained by its battle with China's formal institutional environment and they decided to terminate their Chinese operation (Cell III).

Company H relies heavily on the technology it develops in-house (firm-resource oriented) to give it a competitive advantage in international markets. In developed markets such as the UK, USA and Australia, where legal protection of IP is well regulated, a business such as *Company H* can remain competitive by bringing to the table technologies that local firms have not yet developed. Lax IP regulation and enforcement risks this competitive advantage being undermined by local firms which may copy or absorb the technology without rights, permissions or due compensation. The following example, related by a previous company manager from South Africa who had been based in China for more than ten years, illustrates the kinds of problems that *Company H* experienced in China in this regard:

> there was one engineering professor from a famous university in South China, one day he came to my office and he was a sort of friendly contact to our company. When he showed me his imitated product model of

our machines, I was so angry and shocked that a professor could be so flagrant and ignorant. He did not realise what he had done had infringed our IPR, and he did not feel guilty or shameful, in fact he was actually quite proud of what he had managed to achieve. I was totally speechless.

The engineering professor's department had 'reverse engineered' several items of machinery supplied by *Company H* without even thinking for a moment that intellectual property issues may have been at stake. *Company H* was not entirely naïve about the institutional environment it was entering in China with regard to IP protection, and this strongly influenced their decision to avoid the JV model in favour of setting up a WOFE. But it was other aspects of the localisation process, particularly sealing business deals with local partners proved to be their undoing. *Company H's* core business principle was that it would not sell machinery to its business partners but would instead allow them to use their machinery as contractors. This strategy had worked in other developing markets by obviating the possibility of technology transfer. In China, the strategy failed to achieve its underlying objective. First local firms started producing facsimiles of *Company H's* machinery and technologies. *Company H* thought this was a manageable problem, but it escalated when larger SOEs started doing the same. This was when the company felt it had to move to protect its IP through the Chinese courts. This was not a straightforward process, not only because of the limitations of China's IP legislation but also because state actors often interfered in the legal process on the SOEs' behalf.

Quite soon after entering the Chinese market, *Company H* started to sue the Chinese partners who had imitated their products and technologies. Over the course of ten years, *Company H* attended court hearings at all levels (local, provincial, national) and across half of the nation in different geographical regions and at various administrative levels. Of all the patent infringement cases *Company H* had to fight, one case against three Chinese SOEs at the same time was the most frustrating and time-consuming. Initially, the Superior Court in Province A made a judgement that *Company H* had won the case and that the Chinese defendants were liable to pay compensation to *Company H* and also court costs. But then one of the SOEs counterclaimed, to a different institution (the Patent Reexamination Board of SIPO, the 'Board' for short) and the Intermediate Court in Beijing, that the patents *Company H* held were invalid. Because *Company H* had been unable to provide sufficient proof supporting their own arguments (some of the proof was misrepresented because of inaccurate translations) to the Board and the Court, the Board accepted the Chinese SOE's claim and invalidated *Company H's* patents, and the Intermediate Court also supported the Board's decision.

Company H quickly gathered the requisite proof that they had originally failed to present in the court, and channelled the case to an appropriate legal adviser. In order to challenge the decision made by the two formal Chinese institutions, *Company H* took the Board to the Superior Court. The evidence that *Company H* provided was both comprehensive and sufficient, but *Company H* also benefited from the fact that, in the interim period, China had started to reform its regulatory and supervisory systems relating to IPR. *Company H* was eventually victorious at the Superior Court, defeating the Board's judgement: 'It was a painful process, and from the business point of view we did not win at all. We had to waste so much time and energy on these IPR disputes'. *Company H's* victory in protecting its IP may have helped speed up the process of IP protection reform in China, and will have provided a benchmark that other foreign investing firms could use to their advantage. In some provinces and cities, the cases brought by *Company H* were the first involving IP protection that had ever been heard. Setting up a business in China is relatively straightforward, but negotiating institutional hurdles to consolidating and expanding operations can often be extremely challenging, time-consuming and costly. The financial and emotional cost to *Company H* was so great that it decided to turn its back on the Chinese market and the undoubted possibilities it continues to offer.

3.4 Energy Sector: Business Sometimes Comes Second; Relationship With the Government Is Key

For some types of business investment in China, both foreign and domestic, it is unavoidable to have government stakeholders involved in the business. This particularly applies to strategic sectors such as energy and finance. Whatever the involvement of government stakeholders, the first and most important step for investors to take is to nurture an appropriate and healthy relationship with the government, particularly at the local level. The following two cases will show how the nature of the relationship with local government stakeholders had a profound influence on the China business journey of two South African firms in the energy sector.

Company I is a large global energy and chemical company based in South Africa. The company has developed and holds world-leading coal-to-liquid (CTL) and gas-to-liquid (GTL) technology, and supplies more than a quarter of South Africa's annual fuel requirements. *Company I* was established in 1950 and was maintained as a state-owned enterprise (SOE) until 1979 when it was privatised. One of the largest petrochemical groups in the world, with a sound business model of commercialising cutting-edge technology, *Company I* employs 30,000 people world-wide and operates in more than 30 countries, with particular expertise in developing country contexts.

Despite similarities in the two countries' energy resource profiles,[10] with both China and South Africa possessing much larger reserves of coal than petroleum and thus being ideal locations for the deployment of CTL technologies, *Company I* had steered clear of the Chinese market due to a lack of local knowledge. This changed in 2002 after the then Chinese Prime Minister, Zhu Rongji, invited *Company I* to explore business opportunities in China and to bring its advanced fuel technology to help match energy production to the country's by then very rapid economic development.[11] But, after a ten-year tepid relationship with their un-contracted Chinese partner, *Company I* withdrew its business from China because they were not able to secure approval from the Chinese government on the business co-operation contract they had been expecting and working on for a decade.

Whilst there was great enthusiasm from several Chinese energy companies about the prospect of working with a top-rate international company, not least given the support emanating from the Chinese government, it soon became clear to the managers of *Company I* that the Chinese government wished to be in control of the Chinese companies which would be involved in any future collaboration. One of *Company I's* China country presidents recalled:

> We were almost inundated with (Chinese companies) visits to our head office in Johannesburg . . . but eventually we knew the Chinese government was telling us who we must deal with because we could not make this decision alone.

The signing of an intention to cooperate went smoothly enough, but subsequent business negotiations on the mode of collaboration soon hit rocky ground. Over the ensuing ten years, many things happened, both politically and financially, to both countries and both sets of companies which prevented them from committing to the project according to the agreed schedule. In China, after the central government officials returned from their fact-finding visits to South Africa, it took them 15 months to select two Chinese SOEs (*Company α* and *Company β*) that were believed to match *Company I's* requirements as business partners. Two projects in two provinces were subsequently assigned to *Company I* who then started the first round of feasibility studies. Just four years later, in 2008, when *Company I* was conducting a second round of feasibility studies, a government policy issued by NDRC[12] terminated the co-operation project between *Company I* and *Company α*. Soon afterwards, *Company α* took over *Company β*, placing *Company I's* entire operation in China in jeopardy. The shifting institutional sands halted *Company I's* business development, and added considerable costs to *Company I's* operations, which was very difficult to explain to its shareholders back in South Africa.

In order to secure its last surviving co-operation project in North China, *Company I* sent to China another country president who had been working with *Company I* for 25 years and had vast experience of dealing with foreign joint ventures. Moreover, and perhaps most importantly, the new country president had a more flexible business and communication style than his predecessor, which later proved to be extremely useful when it came to speeding up certain parts of the business development process in China. At the same time, *Company I* decided to set up an office in the province where the project was located with the intention of strengthening relationships with local government officials and partners in order to obtain government approval for the project. In early 2011, *Company I* was granted approval for the project by the Ministry of Ecology and Environment.[13] However, just three months later Chinese *Company α* (*Company I's* business partner-to-be), submitted their own CTL proposal report in which *Company α* proposed to employ China's own CTL technologies, and they were granted government approval within a very short period of time. Although *Company I* had known that China and the Chinese partner were developing their own CTL technology, they believed the project experience that *Company I* had gained over six decades would still prove valuable to the northern China project. At this point the South Africans realised that they were effectively out of the game.

Analysis of Company I's *Chinese Business Strategies Under the 3D Institutional Model*

Company I's entry into the Chinese market was principally driven by the Chinese government, and particularly the seemingly sincere intentions that a high-profile state governor had conveyed to the company (Figure 3.9). At the time, China was in urgent need of the technology that *Company I* could offer. The company was given preferential treatment at the beginning of its business path in China (Cell III), which diminished some of the concerns the company had about entering a new and largely unfamiliar market. Managers of *Company I* determined which products and services they could provide and what business strategies they would deploy in order to optimise the use of their own firm-resources (Cell VI). Confident in their technology and past experience of operating in developing markets, *Company I* entered China (Cell IV), but with a business partner assigned by the Chinese government – a Chinese SOE with local government shareholders. The company had made efforts to familiarise itself with the market through the local 'advisory tanks' (Cell VIII), but they were unable to nurture smooth cooperative relations with the local partner, even though this SOE was a key channel to higher-level government networks, and a lubricant in terms of identifying

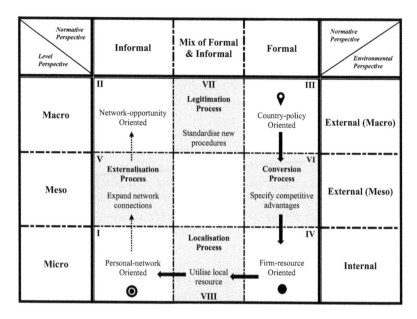

Figure 3.9 Company I's Business Strategies Within the 3D Institutional Model

the key players for the proposed billion-dollar project (Cell V). This externalisation process was actually the ultimate source of *Company I's* failure to consolidate its position within the Chinese energy market.

Company I will have been well aware of the importance of government support in energy sector business development given its earlier experience in South Africa. As a large home-grown SOE, *Company I's* growth during its early years was fundamentally dependent on the South African government's support. Even after privatisation in 1980, the company benefited from state support in the form of tariff protection and subsidies. The encouragement and assurances given to *Company I* by high-level government actors in China led it to believe that it would obtain the requisite government support for a successful venture, and were central to its decision to enter the Chinese market. In the words of the company president:

> We had a look at the regions in the world [for new projects] where the country has coal and water access and has a government who wants to do this. There was also a strategic rationale: the Chinese western regions have got big coal reserves, and the government's intention to develop the western regions of China was quite strong . . . The provincial government also wanted development.

Thus, China's country policy environment appeared to offer a suitable setting for a new business venture. *Company I* also believed that the support of the central and provincial governments would help compensate for the company's own lack of familiarity with the local situation in China, and this was a factor in allowing the government to select the business partners with which *Company I* would collaborate (conversion process). In business parlance, *Company I* chose to compromise its own firm-specific advantage (FSA) in order to obtain a country-specific advantage (CSA). According to Dunning's OLI business framework, any company entering a foreign country market must have ownership (O), location (L) and internalisation (I) advantages. In the case of *Company I*, Location (L) and internalisation (I) advantages were lost through assigning of a business partner and collaboration projects by the government, and all that was left was their specific ownership advantage derived from their technology and experience. *Company I* believed that, by agreeing to this arrangement, they would have a better opportunity to enjoy preferential policies from the central government, thus providing a suitable setting to exploit their remaining firm-specific advantages. On the surface this appeared to be a logical business strategy in the prevailing context, but even with more nuanced local knowledge it would have been difficult for *Company I* to anticipate the shifting policy sands that it eventually encountered.

Shortly after signing the intention to cooperate with the two Chinese partners (*Company α* and *Company β*), *Company I* sent two members of its South African staff to set up a Beijing Office, and at the same time started a first round of project feasibility studies using its own resources and project management experience. The research focused on the physical conditions at the project site and also the prospective business ownership model. *Company I* deployed the same cautious and meticulous business style that it had honed over decades of dealing with both internal shareholders and external stakeholders. Although the first feasibility study delivered encouraging results for the potential projects, there were significant differences of opinion between *Company I* and the Chinese partners on several issues. Of paramount importance to *Company I* was the protection of its IP, which formed the basis of its firm-specific advantage, and accordingly it argued for at least a 50% share of the proposed joint venture. However, the Chinese partner was unwilling to accept such an arrangement. Differences in the respective firms' organisational structures were an additional sticking point. As a private listed company, *Company I* had a responsibility to its shareholders, who were concerned about the likely economic return on their investments. This required a thorough business analysis of the proposed projects. The Chinese SOEs, on the other hand, were attached to the central and regional governments who were driven by the principal political, strategic and security objective of mobilising fuel and energy resources to facilitate regional economic development. In addition, many government officials were involved in the management bodies of these SOEs, which superimposed bureaucratic and hierarchical layers on the decision-making process, as opposed to the time-is-money rationale of *Company I*.

Company I tried to speed things up by replacing the first company president with someone who was considered to have a more flexible business style and who was experienced with foreign joint ventures. His mission was to take responsibility for conducting a second feasibility study and securing approval for the collaborative project from the Chinese government. *Company I* also recruited more local staff, including a local senior manager who had previous experience in the energy industry. In an attempt to ease the communication problems that had blighted the earlier negotiations, the Chinese senior manager built up an advisory team which consisted of consultants from international energy companies, as well as retired directors from Chinese SOEs and academics from relevant institutions (localisation). Informed by the results of the second feasibility study, the advisory team suggested *Company I* should adopt a more flexible approach to negotiations, arguing that offering concessions to the Chinese partners should increase the prospects of obtaining government approval without eating significantly into profit margins. Ultimately, this fresh approach made little difference: it seems the writing was already on the wall. Why was this the case?

According to the 3D institutional framework, after the 'localisation process' *Company I* would be expected to take the step of 'externalisation' by expanding its business communication networks to include connections with higher-echelon stakeholders, typically mediated through local contacts via informal channels. *Company I* in fact adopted a reverse approach during their 'externalisation process'. *Company I's* country president admitted that 'you need senior Chinese staff on your team to help to guide you through, but even the senior Chinese guys here don't know everything. Probably the best route is for you to go through your own government (South Africa) so that they can interact a little bit with Chinese government people to be able to position the project appropriately'. Thus, instead of shortening the communication distance between the company and the Chinese partner, and there through to regional government officials and state regulators – a bottom-up approach – they opted to try to influence matters at central government level to increase leverage on the local situation – a top-down approach. This decision appears to have been taken by *Company I* headquarters. One consequence of deprioritising network-building with the Chinese partner in favour of seeking connections with regional and central officials was that *Company I* was effectively 'out of the loop' when the decision was taken to merge the Chinese *Company α* and *Company β*, which was a consequence of a shift in government policy that *Company I* was unaware of (but could have known about if it had a better relationship with its Chinese partner), and this resulted in *Company I* losing a major project. This reflected shortcomings by *Company I*, in both the externalisation and legitimation processes. The more distant the relationship between *Company I* and the Chinese partner grew, the more difficult it became for them to receive opportunities that the Chinese central government might be in a position to bestow on *Company I*. The Chinese partner was the key mediating conduit to higher-level government officials. 'There is a much stronger role played by the Chinese government in business in China. In a Western country, the government sets the rules and then anybody can play, as long as they follow the rules. In China they set the players as well'. Whilst *Company I* followed the rules to the letter, it did not play well with its assigned player and so eventually faded from the game. Officially, *Company I* claimed it was fluctuations in global oil prices that largely contributed to the unfeasibility of the Chinese CTL project. *Company I* did not leave China altogether as they still maintain some smaller scale business activities in both Hong Kong and the Chinese mainland.

In contrast to *Company I*, **Company J** had a completely different experience in China when dealing with government relationships, experiencing less frustration and showing more understanding and diplomacy, determining that for three decades China has been among their largest consumer markets. *Company J* is one of the largest suppliers of seaborne iron ore in the world, producing more than 80% of the South Africa's iron ore, of which more than 85% is exported to international clients. As a home-grown company in South Africa, *Company J* employs more than 11,500 people, comprising 60% full-time employees and 40% contractors, plus an additional 4,000 fixed-term project contractors on capital expenditure projects in any one year. Although *Company J* has experienced several changes in its ownership structure over the last 40 years, its business strategy with its Chinese clients has remained constant, that is to maintain and continue promoting a cordial relationship.

Company J's first attempt to enter the Chinese markets dates back to the late-1980s, at a time when South Africa was experiencing a crucial period of transformation in domestic social and economic systems, and when China was at the very earliest stages of its policy of opening-up. Whilst the initial articulation of *Company J* and its Chinese clients might initially have appeared implausible given the two countries' quite different ideologies at the time, the relationships that *Company J* has fostered with Chinese partners over the past three decades have contributed *Company J's* principal source of business revenue.

Whilst relationship-building may have been keen to the stability and success of *Company J's* Chinese venture, a fundamental factor in opening the door to the company's business involvement in China was *Company J's* product – high-grade iron ore, with an iron (Fe) content higher than 65% – which was a resource China urgently needed to fuel and maintain its industrialisation process. *Company J* was one of the first South African companies to set up business in China. They sent their first sales team to China in 1988, and within a year had managed to quadruple their sales volume. The turning point to even larger volumes of trade with China occurred in 1994, when *Company J* was able to agree a special arrangement with a local Chinese port authority which was keen to develop their then small seaport and into a major, modern ore transfer port. *Company J's* marketing team leader, excited at the prospect of increasing the company's business in China, convinced *Company J's* headquarters to enter into a joint investment in the port development project with the local port authority. So successful was the venture that *Company J* now exports more than 60% of its annual production to China.

Analysis of Company J's *Chinese Business Strategies Under the 3D Institutional Model*

As with several of the South African firms that have featured in these case studies, a long history of operating in different, and sometimes challenging institutional environments had equipped *Company J* with the resilience and flexibility to adapt to the Chinese institutional setting, aided in no small measure by offering a premium commodity that was in very high demand in post-reform China (Cell IV), which is likely to have opened institutional doors which might otherwise have been difficult to unlock (Figure 3.10). Company J invested heavily in nurturing (Cell I), through both informal and formal channels, good relations with mainland Chinese SOE clients who were mainly local and regional government officials, who then provided a conduit to high-level institutional players (Cell II). Having an initial trade presence in China was also paramount to *Company J's* later business success, as they were on the ground when a local government was looking to up-grade their city's port.

Company J was established as part of South Africa's first state-owned steel corporation, which played a key role in the country's industrial development. With the end of the Apartheid regime in South Africa and the subsequent easing of international sanctions, the country's attention shifted towards finding export markets for South African iron ore. *Company J* was privatised, then subsequently taken over by an international mining conglomerate, and then later unbundled from this corporation and subsequently listed on the JSE to underpin its strategic international business development. But even before the end of the Apartheid era, *Company J* had managed to establish a presence in China, which was one of very few developing countries willing to

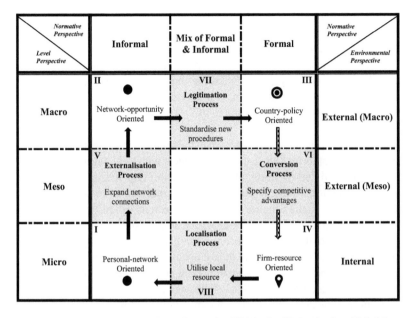

Figure 3.10 Company J's Business Strategies Within the 3D Institutional Model

conduct business with South Africa at the time. Through their Hong Kong sales office, where they employed local Chinese staff to compensate for deficiencies in local knowledge (localisation), *Company J* was able to establish a gateway to mainland China, although this was not without difficulties:

> It was during the dark Apartheid days in South Africa, and South Africa still had diplomatic relationship with Taiwan. China was the 'dangerous Red Country' that we should not get involved with. Our people went to China during those days before cell phones or any advanced electronic communications were freely available, and they disappeared for two weeks into the country. We did not know what happened in those weeks, maybe some were kidnapped, maybe in jail, but it was during those days when we established our relationships with China [our Chinese customers]. They [our people] came back, and they had had a lot of banquets, and fostered good relationships around banquet tables, and those relations still hold strong today – 30 years later.

With their experience of sending their first company staff to China, as described above by *Company J's* research manager, together with their confidence they had in their own products, the platform was established for a successful business venture in China.

It was not long after their entry into China that *Company J* had an opportunity to work jointly on the large seaport project in an east coast city.

> They [the Chinese local authority] came to us with this dream – that one day they wanted this city to become a big iron-importing port! They also said they did not want the 'big three',[14] because those companies were very aggressive, and they did not have friendly relationships with them, so they came to us.

The manager recalled the situations when they initially made contact with the local city port authority. Due to their involvement with local government in this project, the local Port Authority offered *Company J* very special arrangements and good facilities. This generous gesture confirmed again just how important relationships are to the Chinese in China. To a certain extent *Company J* was very fortunate to set up these relations at such an early stage – if they had had to wait until the end of economic sanctions it might have been a slightly different story – but there is no doubt that their emphasis on forming and maintaining good interpersonal relations was an important factor in the smooth progress of the business relationship with China. To foster and maintain their relationships with Chinese clients, *Company J* keep some of its engineers on-site year-round in their Chinese co-operative projects so that they would be there to solve any technical problems which occurred during production. Working teams from both sides (China and South Africa) even visited each other on an annual basis to enhance communication and mutual understanding.

Such an emphasis on networking and relationship-building by *Company J* proved to be advantageous to other elements of the company's business in China. In addition to exporting iron ore to China, *Company J* had various joint ventures operating in Hong Kong to look after steel sales, and the company was also active in looking for further opportunities to collaborate with local Chinese firms. Through their SOE connections, *Company J* was able to build business networks with various stakeholders (externalisation), which in turn enabled them to approach higher-level institutional connections (network opportunity oriented). As the first large South African firm to do business in China, *Company J* was able to build up 'local knowledge' and interpersonal networks over a long period of time, one advantage being that these informal (and formal) channels were crucial sources of knowledge about the prevailing regulatory and legal situations in China and the most effective ways of navigating this institutional environment. However, during the course of *Company J's* nearly four decades of involvement in China, the rules-based institutional setting has evolved and, from the perspective of foreign firms operating in China, improved. As such, the company these days needs to rely less on informal arrangements to lubricate its business dealings in China, and instead must comply more rigidly with formal rules and regulations (legitimisation). *Company J's* ownership structure adds a further imperative to this regime of compliance, its stock exchange listing and accountability to shareholders determining that its business operations are always under constant public scrutiny.

Notes

1. In order to protect the identity of the study firms and to honour undertakings of confidentiality, all study firms will be referred to by letters, here *Company A* and *Company B*.
2. Whilst South Africa has so far failed to achieve preferential trading status for its wine exports to China, it has benefited considerably, indirectly, by China's imposition in November 2020 of punitive tariffs on Australian wine imports, ranging from 107% to 212%.
3. New Zealand and Chilean wine enjoys tax-free status in China, whereas although South Africa has Most Favoured Nation status, the Chinese government still levies an 8% tariff on South African wine imports.
4. *Company C* proposed to purchase 24.99% of the Chinese company's shares at the end of 2009, but by law was not allowed to own more than 20% as a singular investor according to a new policy issued in early 2010 by CIRC. In 2018, CBIRC removed this cap on foreign investors, and *Company C* increased its shareholding to 24.99%.
5. The firm was in fact established as an insurance brokerage in the 1960s before later selling its own insurance products and services from 1980.
6. According to China's regulations on foreign financial institutions entering China, these companies must operate as a non-profit Representative Office for at least two years to up to five years after entry before they are allowed to become a for-profit venture. The State Council amended the policy in 2019, removing this requirement. www.gov.cn/zhengce/2019-10/16/content_5440387.htm (in Chinese, accessed on 30 April 2021).
7. FESCO was the first company established in China in 1979 to provide professional human resources services to foreign enterprises' representative offices, foreign financial institutions and economic organizations in China.
8. *Company E* was involved in negotiations with one British bank at the time, but the latter required more shareholdings than *Company E* could accept. *Chinese Bank X* was in contact with another South African 'four pillar' bank (albeit smaller than *Company E* by assets), but the latter's shareholders rejected the deal offered by *Chinese Bank X*.
9. *Chinese Bank X* had in the region of 290 million retail and 3 million business customers worldwide.
10. Both China and South Africa have more coal reserves than oil.
11. The invitation followed a research visit to *Company I* in early 2000 by five senior Chinese scientists and officials from the Chinese energy sector.
12. National Development and Reform Commission, PRC.
13. Formerly the Ministry of Environmental Protection, State Council of the PRC.
14. The world's top three iron ore suppliers are from Brazil (1) followed by Australia (2).

4 Conclusion

Chapter 3 presented the case studies of ten South African firms, arranged according to the industries and sectors in which they operated within the Chinese market. The case study firms constituted approximately one-third of all South African business firms which had engaged with the Chinese market at the time of the research. The five pairs of study cases highlighted the business strategies employed as these South African firms initially engaged and later consolidated their operations in China. Although there was no objective judgement of 'right' or 'wrong' in relation to these business strategies, it was quite evident that some were more effective than others in underpinning business success in China in both the short and longer terms.

In line with the underlying objectives of this research, key institutional factors and processes, both formal and informal, have provided the principal focus for this investigation of South African firms' business strategies in China. The enquiry has been facilitated by a three-dimensional institutional model which, as well as providing a framework for the analysis of business strategy, has also been tested through its application to these real-world cases and found to be reasonably robust, not least in its flexibility in accommodating a diverse range of business strategies and institutional practices. Despite operating in what would appear, superficially, to be a universal formal institutional setting in China, as introduced in Chapter 2, the case studies reveal that none of the paired firms charted the same entry and consolidation 'path' as hypothesised by the model. One key take-away from the research is that an ability to navigate the informal institutional environment is crucial to business success in China.

4.1 Key Findings

One significant pitfall in international business is the notion, still surprisingly widely held, that the core principles of capitalist economy are the fundamental determinants of success and failure: that 'business is business'.

DOI: 10.4324/9781003165668-4

This study has hopefully shown that 'context counts', and also that the ingredients of business success are multifarious, subtle and, frequently, qualitative. Key generalised descriptors of China, such as 'open doors', 'socialist market economy', 'centralised polity' and 'rules-based economy' require considerable and nuanced unpacking. The following section will distil some of the key findings from this research, and will reflect on the distinctively South African flavour to the management issues faced by the companies which feature in the empirical component of this study.

Firstly, the foreign market location was not necessarily a critical initial concern to these pioneering South African firms when they first ventured to invest overseas (Klein and Wöcke, 2007), so for many of the study firms China was not necessarily the market they specifically targeted for business expansion, but rather was part of a process of organic growth and international business expansion. This was something of a double-edged sword: on the one hand, a lack of contextual knowledge created a very steep learning curve as firms added China to their international business profiles, but on the other, prior experience of operating in developing country markets, where informal business practices are often the norm, may have prepared these firms to adjust to the contextual realities they faced in China.

Secondly, the non-location-oriented nature of the investment drove the South African firms to be more dependent on their own *firms' specific advantages* (FSA) in order to compete and survive in the foreign markets. Sometimes 'no turning back' was the only and best motivation for these firms to contend and survive by developing their own competitiveness in the foreign markets, especially a market such as China which held plenty of unpredictability and uncertainty. Some of the FSAs were inherited from their own home country markets, which had enabled them to sustain themselves and thrive within the domestic markets, but nonetheless these FSAs needed to be further strengthened and new FSAs developed in order to serve the specific needs and character of these foreign markets. In the Chinese markets they also needed to learn and make efforts to protect their own intellectual property in case it might be infringed by local competitors or partners, thereby eroding their own FSA, because China then had (and still has) rather weak and immature institutional mechanisms to protect intellectual property.

Thirdly, the South African managers in general seemed to possess the capability of being able to envision long-term business targets and implement accurate business strategies based on their *business visionary*. Many South African managers were rather inexperienced in terms of involvement in foreign international market environments by the late 1980s due to their isolation because of economic sanctions. However, their ability to perceive risks and their willingness to confront and deal with risks by adapting

themselves and adopting flexible business strategies gave them the competitiveness to contest in foreign markets. There is no doubt that these business
leaders had accumulated confidence and experience from their dominant
position in and experience of operating within a difficult domestic market
in their home country. Many large companies preferred to maintain their
own South African expatriates in the foreign markets to manage and operate
their subsidiaries, including in the Chinese markets where language, culture and communications were (and still are) significant 'stumbling blocks'
for foreigners (Story, 2010, 102), whilst levels of English proficiency and
exposure to 'western culture' had not by then been widely covered in the
education system nor broadly accepted in Chinese society during the early
days of the economic transformation. Therefore, the hindrances and challenges that South African managers' business strategies faced at that time in
the Chinese markets were multifaceted: they had to survive in a seemingly
contradictory foreign market where socialist policies coloured the 'market
economy', ostensibly because they had little choice but to expand and grow
beyond their home markets; the managers had to be able to foresee market
risks even though it was hard to see clearly what exactly the risks were, and
at what point these risks might manifest as a real crisis for the business, and
at which point loss-minimisation also became crucial; and the managers
had to learn to find a way to communicate with the local market in the local
'language'.

Last but not least, *local market dominance* remains critical for South
African firms even after they become global leaders in their own sectors.
Companies such as SAB Miller, which have become leading international
enterprises based in part upon their own internationalised South African
label (with a blurred distinction between the domestic and the international), nonetheless rely for their dominant position in their strong domestic
market which still contributes a large portion of their overall profits, while
Research and Development (R&D) facilities which are retained in the home
country continue to provide the firm with the know-how needed to maintain
their competitive advantage in the foreign markets.

The principal, and I think quite important, conclusion to be drawn from
these case studies is that it is quite dangerous to generalise the way in which
the prevailing political economy (of both host and home country) affects
business processes and outcomes. The background discussion in Chapter 1
is of necessity somewhat generalised, although it is sufficiently nuanced to
convey the sense that not all South African firms are the same – they vary by
size, sector, history, geographical location and institutional connectivity –
nor is the economic landscape that faces them in China uniform. Nonetheless, a number of factors have been identified that would appear to affect
South African business firms entering the Chinese markets in a similar if

not identical manner. These include prior experience of using informal institutional channels, prior international business experience, experience of negotiating state bureaucracy and policy interference in the 'free' market (and associated social agendas), the degree of enforced self-reliance, unfamiliarity with weaknesses in the formal institutional system and the way that political realities have affected the timing of market entry in China. The cross-sectional case studies show that South African firms are extremely variable in terms of their home country profile and experience, the nature and degree of their previous exposure to international markets, the level and extent to which they engage with both formal institutional structures and engage in informal institutional practices, and both their degree of understanding of the complexities of the Chinese markets and their preparedness (and in some cases willingness) to adapt their business models accordingly. But I think one of the key differences between these firms can be attributed to what I would call the 'personality of the firm'. Businesses, ultimately, consist of people, and people go about their business in quite different ways. Some of the business managers were very flexible and open-minded about doing business in China while others were quite stubborn and even dogmatic. The firms which recognised that there is no single model for success in international business, and that China required a particular mind-set and methodology, and which inserted into their operations business managers who understood China (and Chinese language and culture), or which took the time to nurture good relations with their Chinese counterparts – these were the firms that appeared to enjoy more success, or at least a less bumpy ride, than others who did less to invest in the personal software of international business.

4.2 A South African Business Flavour?

How do the case study firms' business strategies compare with those of the large established South African firms which entered the Chinese market before 1994, given that both countries have experienced a thoroughgoing process of socio-economic transformation over the last two decades, and China has by now has become a more 'mature' destination for foreign investment compared with 30 years ago? One of the challenges that this research faced was the lack of primary research resources on large established South African firms (e.g. AAC, SAB, Sappi, etc.) which had invested in the Chinese markets before 1994. A limited amount of quality research had been conducted (e.g. Klein and Wöcke, 2007; Feinstein, 2005; Feinstein, 2007; Horwitz *et al.*, 2005; Correia and Chung, 2007), and this work, together with reports from various corporates and groups, has provided useful secondary material to allow me to engage this question.

Presuming that large numbers of South African firms had been able to enter the Chinese markets at the beginning of the Chinese 'open door' policy introduced in the late 1970s, and presuming also that at the same time South Africa had not been under the dark shadow of the Apartheid era, how different might the South African firms' business strategies have been compared to those described in the case studies? The answer is that they would possibly not have differed much from those of firms from the US or Western Europe. This is because the advanced macro-level institutional systems and arrangements in South Africa were quite similar to those familiar to Western firms, and thus they would have entered the Chinese market with broadly similar tools and experience gleaned from operating historically in foreign markets. Such a view is supported by the fact that the overseas foreign direct investment (OFDI) of South African firms ranked amongst the highest in international comparison by the late 1960s and early 1970s (Feinstein, 2005). However, for reasons found principally in the realm of international relations, most of the South African firms presented in my research case studies entered China at a point in time after both countries, China and South Africa, had already experienced thoroughgoing processes of transition and reform. This obliged the South African firms to adjust their own business strategies not only in the host country markets, but also first in their home country market.

South Africa over time formed a somewhat solid and robust macro-level institutional system which directed and guided the country's economic development for at least half a century. But since the ANC gained power and leadership responsibilities, they have steered the country in a quite different direction, prioritising economic restructuring, the elimination of poverty and inequality, and the generation of employment. This has required the building of a somewhat different institutional system at the micro-, meso- and macro-levels – a process that is still far from complete and, debatably, continues to provide hurdles to the reform process as well as economic development (Mangcu, 2012). What have been the implications of this for South African business, and the way that South African firms operate in the Chinese markets?

Unlike those large established South African firms who were the pioneers in exploring the international markets, most South African domestic firms first began to adjust their products and services to the 'local' African markets, in the process learning to deal with the risks found in markets where the (especially micro) institutional system was weak or even chaotic, such as by gaining skills and experience of building business-related social networks with upper-level institutional players in order to offset the inefficiencies and challenges that the unpredictable institutional environment presented to them.

Whilst it is difficult to prove empirically, it is reasonable to suggest that this unique (in the sense of its political drivers) domestic experience serendipitously prepared those South African firms which later ventured into the Chinese market to cope with a similarly unpredictable and flexible institutional environment. Whilst the underlying story of China's remarkable economic growth is by now very well known, and the political platform upon which it has been built has been quite solid, the inner workings of the system – at both the macro- and micro-levels – can hardly be described as cast in stone. Foreign business in particular requires a certain nimbleness, astuteness and contextual awareness to be able to retain a stable stance on fluid and flexible foundations (Story, 2010), and the case studies (in the main, but not universally) suggest that South African firms' experience of operating in a similar political-economic environment has given them a distinctive, and I contend a distinctively South African flavour to their operations in the Chinese markets. 'Location' may still not seem to be the necessary key factor to every case study of South African firm, but the firms offering retail and financial products would definitely look into the right market locations in China where the consumers would have the capacity to accept and purchase their products.

There has additionally been an extra layer of challenge that South African firms have had to contend with, as most of them entered the Chinese markets at a relatively late stage compared with most Western firms (except for the big South African investors and conglomerates which entered China at the end of the Apartheid era, mostly associated with 'capital flight' from the Republic). The disadvantage of being a latecomer to the Chinese markets required the firms to offer products, services and/or skills that were in high demand or were especially needed in China. The investigation of South African firms in my case studies has shown that the ones that have been able to survive and operate effectively in the Chinese markets to date have offered products/service that are either/both innovative or distinctive and thus desirable and acceptable to the Chinese. In other words, the strong FSAs are still a source of competitiveness for South African firms which can depend on the home country to help them contest the host county market. IP protection can still be an issue that some South African firms (e.g. case study of *Company H*) find difficulty with in the Chinese markets, even though China has seen some improvement since WTO entry in terms of institutional regulations and legitimation. Some companies had less concern (e.g. case study of *Company C* and *D*) about IP, but this was not because they were not fearful of losing their IP, rather it was mainly because the products/service they offered to the Chinese markets would have effectiveness for only a given period of time in these markets, and before the current products/services could be 'stolen' new ones would come into the markets to replace the old ones due to their continuous innovation derived from their home country markets.

Finally, we have also seen that these South African firms have a generally higher awareness of the unpredictability of the Chinese markets, and thus they have been willing to adopt somewhat flexible business strategies, in much the same way as they do in their home and African markets, in order to manage their business operations in such markets. By setting up business partnerships with local firms in order to use their local social and business networks, and in particular their willingness to make an effort to build relationships with upper-level institutional contacts as well as using networks to function effectively at the micro-level in China, they have helped to enhance the efficiency and effectiveness of their respective businesses. Whilst it is not intended to infer that firms from other countries have not also functioned in a similar manner at the macro- and micro-levels, both the timing and the political contexts within which they have operated have created a distinctive set of environmental and circumstantial factors surrounding South African firms' entry into and consolidation within the Chinese markets.

4.3 Contributions to the Study of International Business

The core focus of this book is the interaction, interfacing and interplay of private sector firms and public sector institutions, which occurs on a range of levels from the state down to the city and locality, and at the macro- down to the micro-scale. These interactions take place across time (with bridge-headers establishing an experiential platform for latecomers to benefit from, or gaining a competitive advantage over late arrivals), involve negotiating a shifting institutional landscape, and may be based on different permutations of formal and informal institutional contact. We have mainly been concerned with the internal factors that are specific to both the firms in question and the institutions with which they interact, but it has also emerged from the discussion that there are processes and arrangements external to this that also have some bearing on the dynamics and outcomes of these firm-institution interactions.

In the first chapter we can identify some of the elements which, loosely, map out the historical and political parameters of political economy, and provide the wider contextual setting within which this story is placed. From a nationalistic agenda which is shaded by political ideology emerge particular arrays of policies, laws, rules and regulations which are the main institutional structures and hurdles that foreign-investing firms must negotiate, perhaps with the assistance of agents or partners who bridge or smooth the path. We have seen that, however rigid these 'rules of the game' may appear on paper, there is room for translation, interpretation and even negotiation within the 'realeconomy'. Informal business and institutional practices, underwritten or lubricated by *guanxi*, socialising, connections, contacts, networks and relationships, and perhaps translated cross-culturally by local staff, are often the space where such 'wriggle room' is found or created.

My conceptual and analytical model (the 3D Institutional Model) is presented as my main contribution to the existing body of knowledge in the field of International Business. The model is used to analyse and explain how firms use 'institutions' as navigation tools to enter, penetrate and operate in the Chinese market. Following the advice of Buckley and Casson (2009, 1575), who called for IB studies to have 'a dynamic new agenda' to investigate the development of MNEs in a more flexible form, the 3D Institutional Model displays a dynamic motion of firms in each business stage, including the business strategies they have employed. I hope also that the model might be of some value in the real world, as firms consider the business strategies they might use to chart a path through the range of business and institutional hurdles and challenges they may encounter on entering and consolidating their position within foreign markets, whilst remaining mindful of the specificities of case and context.

The rationale for the 3D Institutional Model is drawn from a mix of existing classic international business studies theories, but it has been developed and refined based on empirical and contextual insight. Theoretically, the classic international business study theories and models, which I have reviewed in Chapter 2, have largely been developed from analysing the business experiences of multinational enterprises from developed markets (e.g. the US, Europe and Japan), and are valuable in helping to understand the early phases of business investment in foreign markets. In contrast, firms from developing source markets have come to constitute a later phase in cross-border business investment, and it is not altogether certain that the classic business models are powerful or flexible enough to explain fully and represent these firms' transnational business activities. The present study rises to IB scholars' call for an evolution of traditional business frameworks. For instance, Rugman and others (2011) have suggested a shift in perspective when applying his classic business model (FSA/CSA Matrix), away from the original focus on the home country's CSA, towards focusing more attention on CSAs generating from home country/region markets and their affective relations with FSA. These perspectives have been included in the 3D Institutional Model in the form of the environmental perspective: internal institutions.

In addition, this model has further advanced and emphasised the importance of 'institutions' in the investigation of business activities in emerging and developing markets – an increasingly fashionable business research perspective over the last decade or so – following on from the pioneering work in Mike Peng's (various years) 'Institutional Perspective Approach' and Han Jansson's 'Institutional Network Approach' (Jansson, 2007). The 3D Institutional Model has in particular been inspired by these IB scholars' approach to engage with institutional studies, informed by various institutional stances to form the initial building blocks of 3D Institutional Model.

The second contribution of this research, which follows on from the first, concerns the analytical framework which is created by the three-dimensional perspectives of my institutional model, in which each set of dimensional elements interacts with and is affected by other elements. The 'four-stage transforming process' shows both the continuity and fluidly of firms' business development progression and the business strategies they may take to extend their business path. 'Institution' is used as a navigation tool to guide and even guard them in choosing 'appropriate' business strategies (although not all of my case study firms in fact took the 'right' path). There is no doubt that this study model could be further advanced and refined through additional and broader empirical research, but in its present form it does at least bring a dynamic dimension to our understanding of firms' point of entry into transnational business. My present study scratches beneath the surface of real business stories and situations, in a way that a generalised model would find it difficult to accomplish, and thus I hope that the rich and rare empirical insight provided by my case studies of South African firms entering the Chinese markets might be considered the third contribution made by my research work.

Lastly, this is one of very few research studies to focus on South African OFDI to China. It has managed to cover a good percentage (around 25% during the research period, based on the available firm data statistics) of South African firms operating in the Chinese market. This research has been one of the first (to my knowledge) to investigate and provide qualitative insight into South African firms' business strategies in the Chinese market. In addition, the 3D institutional model seems able to explain 'why' South African firms invest in the Chinese market, and most importantly 'how' and 'what' strategies these firms have employed in order to help them enter, operate and consolidate their position within the Chinese markets. The model also hopefully provides a tool for other researchers to use and test empirically in other developing markets.

4.4 Suggestions for Further Research

Intuitively, I have come to believe, through this research, that although theoretical literature places quite heavy emphasis on formal institutional environments and processes, what really makes things happen and keeps things moving lies in those elements and practices that I have termed, perhaps a little too generically, 'informal'. A bearing without a lubricant sooner or later seizes up. With more time, it would have been nice to unpack the notion of 'informal' in order to reveal even more complexity and diversity than this book has been able to show and elaborate. As my 3D Institutional Model suggests, there is no clear binary between formal and informal; the connection between the two would best be seen as a continuum. Future research might attempt to theorise and operationalise this continuum, and also explore it internationally across business settings.

Another objective of this research has been to attempt to weave several disciplinary perspectives into a field of study that historically has been claimed quite narrowly by IB and/or IPE. I lack the disciplinary training in, say, Anthropology or Sociology, or perhaps Cultural Studies, to leave my parent disciplines too far behind, but I have been convinced by this research that the complexity and diversity of the world in which we live is such that there can no longer be any effective place for disciplines that define themselves as 'silos' separate from other fields of knowledge. I know I have not invested enough interdisciplinary research in this project, and I recognise that many scholars have already been venturing into this territory since my research was initiated, but the fluidity and diversity of processes, situations and outcomes that my research has highlighted reinforces, in my own mind, the value of transdisciplinary and qualitative research into international business processes and outcomes.

References

Abdulai, David, 2017, *Chinese Investment in Africa: How African Countries Can Position Themselves to Benefit From China's Foray Into Africa*, London: Routledge.

Abegunrin, Olayiwola and Charity Manyeruke, 2020, *China's Power in Africa: A New Global Order*, Cham, Switzerland: Palgrave.

Abiru, Fadekemi, 2018, "Africa's Lost Decade: Women and the Structural Adjustment Programme", *The Republic*, 25 September.

Adelzadeh, Asghar, 1996, "From the RDP to GEAR: The Gradual Embracing of Neo-Liberalism in Economic Policy", *Transformation*, No. 31, 66–95.

Adem, Seifudein, 2014, *China's Diplomacy in Eastern and Southern Africa*, London: Routledge.

Aguilera, Ruth V. and Birgitte Grøgaard, 2019, "The Dubious Role of Institutions in International Business: A Road Forward", *Journal of International Business Studies*, 50, 1, 20–35.

Alden, Chris, 2007, *China in Africa*, London: Zed Books.

Alden, Chris and Cristina Alves, 2008, "History and Identity in the Construction of China's Africa Policy", *Review of African Political Economy*, 35, 115, 43–58.

Alden, Chris and Daniel Large, 2019, *New Directions in Africa-China Studies*, Abingdon: Routledge.

Alexander, Neville, 2007, "Affirmative Action and the Perpetuation of Racial Identities in Post-Apartheid South Africa", *Transformation*, No. 63, 92–126.

Ampiah, Kweku and Sanusha Naidu, eds., 2008, *Crouching Tiger, Hidden Dragon? Africa and China*, Scottsville: University of KwaZulu-Natal Press.

ANC, 1992, *Ready to Govern: ANC Policy Guidelines for a Democratic South Africa*, www.anc1912.org.za/policy-documents-1992-ready-to-govern-anc-policy-guidelines-for-a-democratic-south-africa/.

April, Funeka Yazini and Garth Shelton, eds., 2014, *Perspectives on South Africa-China Relations at 15 Years*, Pretoria: Africa Institute of South Africa.

Berger, Peter L. and Thomas Luckmann, 1967, *The Social Construction of Reality*, Garden City, NY: Anchor Books.

Bodomo, Adams, 2019, "Africa-China-Europe Relations: Conditions and Conditionalities", *Journal of International Studies*, 12, 4, 115–129.

Bopela, Thula, 2009, "Why Some People Are Turning on the Party of the Poor Once They Are Through the Door of Opportunity", *Friends of Jacob Zuma Website*, 21 January.

Buckley, Peter J. and Mark C. Casson, 1976, *The Future of the Multinational Enterprise*, London: Macmillan.

Buckley, Peter J. and Mark C. Casson, 2002, *The Future of the Multinational Enterprise* (25th Anniversary Edition), Basingstoke: Palgrave Macmillan.

Buckley, Peter J. and Mark C. Casson, 2009, "The Internalisation Theory of the Multinational Enterprise: A Review of the Progress of a Research Agenda after 30 Years", *Journal of International Business Studies*, 40, 9, 1563–1580.

Burt, Ronald Stuart, 1992, *Structural Holes: The Social Structure of Competition*, Cambridge, MA: Harvard University Press.

Cameron, Robert, 1996, "The Reconstruction and Development Programme", *Journal of Theoretical Politics*, 8, 2, 283–294.

Carlisle, Elliot and Dave Flynn, 2005, "Small Business Survival in China: Guanxi, Legitimacy, and Social Capital", *Journal of Developmental Entrepreneurship*, 10, 1, 79–96.

Carmody, Pádraig Risteard, 2016, *The New Scramble for Africa* (2nd Edition), Cambridge: Polity Press.

Carmody, Pádraig Risteard, Peter Kragelund and Ricardo Reboredo, 2020, *Africa's Shadow Rise: China and the Mirage of African Economic Development*, London: Zed Books.

Chaffee, John W., 2018, *The Muslim Merchants of Premodern China: The History of a Maritime Asian Trade Diaspora, 750–1400*, Cambridge: Cambridge University Press.

Chang, Kuei-Sheng, 1970, "Africa and the Indian Ocean in Chinese Maps of the Fourteenth and Fifteenth Centuries", *Imago Mundi*, 24, 21–20.

Chang, Kuei-Sheng, 1974, "The Maritime Scene in China at the Dawn of Great European Discoveries", *Journal of the American Oriental Society*, 94, 3, 347–359.

Chen, J., 2013, "全球冷战与中国漫长的崛起", 冷战国际史研究, 9, 1, 27–42.

Chin, Gregory T. and B. Michael Frolic, 2007, *Emerging Donors in International Development Assistance: The China Case*, Ottawa: International Development Research Centre, Partnership and Business Development Division.

Corder, Clive K., 1997, "The Reconstruction and Development Programme: Success or Failure?", *Social Indicators Research*, 41, 1/3, 183–203.

Correia, G.N. and R. Chung, 2007, "The World's Largest Brewer in the World's Largest Market: A Strategic Analysis of InBev's Expansion to China", MBA thesis, Boston: Harvard Business School.

Davies, Howard, *et al.*, 1995, "The Benefits of 'Guanxi': The Value of Relationships in Developing the Chinese Market", *Industrial Marketing Management*, 24, 3, 207–214.

Davies, Ken, 2012, "Inward Foreign Direct Investment in China and Its Policy Context", *China: An International Journal*, 10, 1, 62–74.

Davies, Martyn, *et al.*, 2008, *How China Delivers Development Assistance to Africa*, Centre for Chinese Studies, Stellenbosch: University of Stellenbosch.

Deloitte, 2020, 开放政策下外资险企 在中国的新机遇, www2.deloitte.com/cn/zh/pages/financial-services/articles/china-market-opportunities-for-foreign-insurance-companies-under-the-new-opening-up-policies.html.

DiMaggio, Paul J. and Walter W. Powell, 1983, "The Iron Cage Revisited: Institutional Isomorphism and Collective Rationality in Organizational Fields", *American Sociological Review*, 48, 2, 147–160.

DiMaggio, Paul J. and Walter W. Powell, 1991, *The New Institutionalism in Organizational Analysis*, Chicago: University of Chicago Press.

Doh, Jonathan, *et al.*, 2017, "International Business Responses to Institutional Voids", *Journal of International Business Studies*, 48, 3, 293–307.

Dollar, David, 2019, "Understanding China's Belt and Road Infrastructure Projects in Africa", Brookings Institution, John L. Thornton China Center, Global China: Assessing China's Growing Role in the World.

Doz, Yves, 2011, "Qualitative Research for International Business", *Journal of International Business Studies*, 42, 5, 582–590.

Dreher, Axel and Andreas Fuchs, 2015, "Rogue Aid? An Empirical Analysis of China's Aid Allocation", *The Canadian Journal of Economics*, 48, 3, 988–1023.

Dreyer, Edward L., 2006, *Zheng He: China and the Oceans in the Early Ming Dynasty, 1405–1433*, New York: Pearson, Library of World Bibliography Series.

Dunfee, Thomas W. and Danielle E. Warren, 2001, "Is Guanxi Ethical? A Normative Analysis of Doing Business in China", *Journal of Business Ethics*, 32, 3, 191–204.

Dunning, John H., 1980, "Toward an Eclectic Theory of International Production: Some Empirical Tests", *Journal of International Business Studies*, 11, 1, 9–31.

Dunning, John H., 1988, *Explaining International Production*, London: Unwin Hyman.

Dunning, John H., 2000, "The Eclectic Paradigm as an Envelope for Economic and Business Theories of MNE Activity", *International Business Review*, 9, 2, 163–190.

Dunning, John H. and Sarianna M. Lundan, 2008a, *Multinational Enterprises and the Global Economy* (2nd Edition), Cheltenham: Edward Elgar.

Dunning, John H. and Sarianna M. Lundan, 2008b, "Institutions and the OLI Paradigm of the Multinational Enterprise", *Asia Pacific Journal of Management*, 25, 4, 573–593.

Ellis, Stephen, 2013, *External Mission: The ANC in Exile, 1960–1990*, Oxford: Oxford University Press.

Fan, Ying, 2007, "Gūanxi, Government and Corporate Reputation in China: Lessons for International Companies", *Marketing Intelligence and Planning*, 25, 5, 499–510.

Feinstein, Andrea, 2007, *After the Party: A Personal and Political Journey Inside the ANC*, Johannesburg and Cape Town: Jonathan Ball Publishers.

Feinstein, Charles H., 2005, *An Economic History of South Africa: Conquest, Discrimination and Development*, Cambridge: Cambridge University Press.

Fine, Ben, 2012, "Assessing South Africa's New Growth Path: Framework for Change?", *Review of African Political Economy*, 39, 134, 551–568.

Fine, Ben and Zavareh Rustomjee, 1996, *The Political Economy of South Africa: From Minerals-Energy Complex to Industrialisation*, London: C. Hurst and Co.

Finlay, Robert, 2008, "The Voyages of Zheng He: Ideology, State Power, and Maritime Trade in Ming China", *The Journal of the Historical Society*, 8, 3, 327–347.

FOCAC, 2020, *Stronger China-Africa Ties Key to Post-COVID-19 Economic Recovery*, Beijing: Forum on China-Africa Cooperation.

Gao, Jinyuan, 1984, "China and Africa: The Development of Relations Over Many Centuries", *African Affairs*, 83, 331, 241–250.

Githaiga, Nancy Muthoni, Alfred Burimaso, Wang Bing and Salum Mohammed Ahmed, 2019, "The Belt and Road Initiative: Opportunities and Risks for Africa's Connectivity", *China Quarterly of International Strategic Studies*, 5, 1, 117–141.

Goldsmith, Ronald E., Barbara A. Lafferty and Stephen J. Newell, 2000, "The Impact of Corporate Credibility and Celebrity Credibility on Consumer Reaction to Advertising", *Journal of Advertising*, 29, 3, 43–54.

Gomez-Arias, J. Tomas, 1998, "A Relationship Marketing Approach to Guanxi", *European Journal of Marketing*, 32, 1/2, 145–156.

Gong, Tianyu and Bilian Ni Sullivan, 2017, "Balancing the Power of the State and the Market: A Resource Dependence Perspective on the Role of Government Policies on Firm Innovation in China's Transitional Economy", Annual Meeting of the Academy of Management, 4–8 August, Atlanta, USA.

Government of South Africa, Department of Finance, 1996, *Growth, Employment and Redistribution: A Macroeconomic Strategy*, www.gov.za.

Greve, Arent and Janet W. Salaff, 2003, "Social Networks and Entrepreneurship", *Entrepreneurship, Theory and Practice*, 28, 1, 1–22.

Grimm, Sven, 2014, "China-Africa Cooperation: Promises, Practice and Prospects", *Journal of Contemporary China*, 23, 90, 993–1011.

Guthrie, Douglas, 1998, "The Declining Significance of *Guanxi* in China's Economic Transition", *The China Quarterly*, 154 (June), 254–282.

Hamilton, Carolyn, Bernard K. Mbenga and Robert Ross, eds., 2010, *The Cambridge History of South Africa: From Early Times to 1885*, Cambridge: Cambridge University Press.

Hanauer, Larry and Lyle J. Morris, 2014, *Chinese Engagement in Africa: Drivers, Reactions, and Implications for U.S. Policy*, Santa Monica, CA: RAND Corporation.

Hanlon, Joseph, 1986, *Beggar Your Neighbours: Apartheid Power in Southern Africa*, London: Catholic Institute for International Relations.

Hansen, Eric L., 1995, "Entrepreneurial Networks and New Organization Growth", *Entrepreneurship Theory and Practice*, 19, 4, 7–19.

Haroz, David, 2011, "China in Africa: Symbiosis or Exploitation?", *The Fletcher Forum of World Affairs*, 35, 2, 65–88.

Herbst, Jeffrey, 2005, "Mbeki's South Africa", *Foreign Affairs*, 84, 6 (November–December), 93.

Horwitz, F., M. Ferguson, I. Rivett and A. Lee, 2005, "The Afro-Asian Nexus: South African Multinational Firm Experiences in the Chinese Labour Markets: Key Focus Areas", *South African Journal of Business Management*, 36, 3, 29–40.

Hotho, Jasper J., 2014, "From Typology to Taxonomy: A Configurational Analysis of National Business Systems and their Explanatory Power", *Organization Studies*, 35, 5, 671–702.

Hotho, Jasper J. and Torben Pedersen, 2012, "Beyond the 'Rules of the Game': Three Institutional Approaches and How They Matter for International Business", In: Geoffrey Wood and Mehmet Demirbag, eds., *Handbook of Institutional Approaches to International Business*, Cheltenham: Edward Elgar, 236–273.

Hung, Kineta, Kimmy W. Chan and Calen H. Tse, 2011, "Assessing Celebrity Endorsement Effects in China: A Consumer-Celebrity Relational Approach", *Journal of Advertising Research*, 51, 4, 6–21.

Hutchinson, Alan, 1975, *China's African Revolution*, London: Hutchinson.

Hwang, Dennis B., Patricia L. Golemon, Yan Chen, Teng-Shih Wang and Wen-Shai Hung, 2009, "*Guanxi* and Business Ethics in Confucian Society Today: An Empirical Case Study in Taiwan", *Journal of Business Ethics*, 89, 2, 235–250.

Hybels, Ralph C., 1995, "On Legitimacy, Legitimation, and Organizations: A Critical Review and Integrative Theoretical Model", *Academy of Management Proceedings*, 1995, 1, 241–245.

Hymer, Stephen Herbert, 1960, "The International Operations of National Firms: A Study of Direct Investment", Unpublished PhD thesis, Cambridge: Massachusetts Institute of Technology, Department of Economics.

Ismael, Tareq Y., 1971, "The People's Republic of China and Africa", *The Journal of Modern African Studies*, 9, 4, 507–529.

Jansson, Hans, 2007, *International Business Strategy in Emerging Country Markets: The Institutional Network Approach*, Cheltenham: Edward Elgar.

Jenkins, Rhys, 2019, *How China Is Reshaping the Global Economy: Development Impacts in Africa and Latin America*, Oxford: Oxford University Press.

Jiang, Hua Jie, 2014, "A Study on Chinese Aid to African Countries in the Cold War Era (1960–1978)", Unpublished PhD Dissertation, East China Normal University.

Johanson, Jan and Jan-Erik Vahlne, 1977, "The Internationalization Process of the Firm: A Model of Knowledge Development and Increasing Foreign Market Commitments", *Journal of International Business Studies*, 8, 1, 23–32.

Johanson, Jan and Jan-Erik Vahlne, 2009, "The Uppsala Internationalization Process Model Revisited: From Liability of Foreignness to Liability of Outsidership", *Journal of International Business Studies*, 40, 9, 1411–1431.

Kinra, Aseem and Herbert Kotzab, 2008, "A Macro-Institutional Perspective on Supply Chain Environmental Complexity", *International Journal of Production Economics*, 115, 2, 283–295.

Klein, Saul and Albert Wöcke, 2007, "Emerging Global Contenders: The South African Experience", *Journal of International Management*, 13, 3, 319–337.

Konings, Piet, 2007, "China and Africa: Building a Strategic Partnership", *Journal of Developing Societies*, 23, 3, 341–367.

Kostova, Tatiana and G. Tomas M. Hult, 2016, "Meyer and Peng's 2005 Article as a Foundation for an Expanded and Refined International Business Research Agenda: Context, Organizations, and Theories", *Journal of International Business Studies*, 47, 1, 23–32.

Krapež, Jana, Miha Škerlavaj and Aleš Groznik, 2012, "Contextual Variables of Open Innovation Paradigm in the Business Environment of Slovenian Companies", *Economic and Business Review*, 14, 1, 17–38.

Krug, Barbara and Hans Hendrischke, 2008, "Framing China: Transformation and Institutional Change Through Co-Evolution", *Management and Organization Review*, 4, 1, 81–108.

Kynoch, Gary, 2003, "Controlling the Coolies: Chinese Mineworkers and the Struggle for Labor in South Africa, 1904–1910", *The International Journal of African Historical Studies*, 36, 2, 309–329.

Larsen, Larissa, *et al.*, 2004, "Bonding and Bridging: Understanding the Relationship Between Social Capital and Civic Action", *Journal of Planning Education and Research*, 24, 1, 64–77.

Lee, Ching Kwan, 2017, *The Specter of Global China: Politics, Labor, and Foreign Investment in Africa*, Chicago: University of Chicago Press.

Li, Anshan, 2000, 非洲华侨华人史, Beijing: Zhong Guo Hua Qiao Chu Ban She.

Li, Anshan, 2012a, *A History of Overseas Chinese in Africa to 1911*, New York: Diasporic Africa Press.

Li, Anshan, 2012b, "论中非合作论坛的起源 – 兼谈对中国非洲战略的思考", *Wai jiao xue yuan xue bao = Journal of F.A.C*, 29, 3, 15–32.

Li, Anshan, 2015a, "Contact Between China and Africa Before Vasco da Gama: Archaeology", *Document and Historiography* 世界史研究（英文版）, 2, 1, 34–59.

Li, Anshan, 2015b, "African Diaspora in China: Reality, Research and Reflection", *The Journal of Pan African Studies*, 7, 10, 10–43.

Li, Anshan, 2019, "African Studies in China in the Twenty-First Century: A Historiographical Survey", In: Chris Alden and Daniel Large, eds., *New Directions in Africa-China Studies*, Abingdon: Routledge, 51–72.

Lin, Ying, 2004, "Ruler of the Treasure Country: The Image of the Roman Empire in Chinese Society From the First to the Fourth Century AD", *Latomus*, 63, 2, 327–339.

Lovett, Steve, Lee C. Simmons and Raja Kali, 1999, "Guanxi Versus the Market: Ethics and Efficiency", *Journal of International Business Studies*, 30, 2, 231–247.

Makgetla, Neva and Ann Seidman, 1980, *Outposts of Monopoly Capitalism: Southern Africa in the Changing Global Economy*, Westport, CT: Lawrence Hill and Co.

Mangcu, Xolela, 2012, "Rethinking Africa's Political Economy: An Institutionalist Perspective on South Africa", *Society for International Development*, 55, 4, 477–483.

Manji, Firoze and Stephen Marks, eds., 2007, *African Perspectives on China in Africa*, Oxford: Fahamu, Networks for Social Justice.

Maurer, John G., 1971, *Readings in Organization Theory: Open-System Approaches*, New York: Random House.

Mboweni, Tito Titus, 2004, *The South African Banking Sector – an Overview of the Past 10 Years.* [Speech]. Johannesburg, 14 December 2004, Available from: http://www.bis.org/review/r041231f.pdf

Meyer, Anja and Maryna Steyn, 2016, "Chinese Indentured Mine Labour and the Dangers Associated With Early 20th Century Deep-Level Mining on the

Witwatersrand Gold Mines, South Africa", *International Journal of Osteoarchaeology*, 26, 648–660.

Meyer, Klaus E., Saul Estrin, Sumon Kumar Bhaumik and Mike W. Peng, 2009, "Institutions, Resources, and Entry Strategies in Emerging Economies", *Strategic Management Journal*, 30, 1, 61–80.

Meyer, Klaus E. and Mike W. Peng, 2005, "Probing Theoretically Into Central and Eastern Europe: Transactions, Resources, and Institutions", *Journal of International Business Studies*, 36, 6, 600–621.

Ministry of Foreign Affairs, PRC, 2018, *Beijing Declaration: Toward an Even Stronger China-Africa Community With a Shared Future*, Beijing: Ministry of Foreign Affairs.

Mosala, S.J., J.C.M. Venter and E.G. Bain, 2017, "South Africa's Economic Transformation Since 1994: What Influence Has the National Democratic Revolution (NDR) Had?", *The Review of Black Political Economy*, 44, 3–4, 327–340.

Mthant, Thanti and Kalu Ojah, 2017, "Institutions and Corporate Governance in South Africa", In: Franklin N. Ngwu, Onyeka K. Osuji and Frank H. Stephen, eds., *Corporate Governance in Developing and Emerging Markets*, London: Routledge, 125–139.

Muekalia, Domingos Jardo, 2004, "Africa and China's Strategic Partnership", *African Security Review*, 13, 1, 5–11.

Naughton, Barry, 2008, "The Political Economy of China's Economic Transition", In: Loren Brandt and Thomas Rawski, eds., *China's Great Economic Transformation*, Cambridge: Cambridge University Press, 91–135.

Niew, Shong Tong, 1969, "The Population Geography of the Chinese Communities in Malaysia, Singapore and Brunei", Unpublished PhD thesis, University of London, May.

Nikkel, Michael Irl, 1995, "'Chinese Characteristics' in Corporate Clothing: Questions of Fiduciary Duty in China's Company Law", *Minnesota Law Review*, 80, 2, 503–542.

North, Douglass C., 1990a, *Institutions, Institutional Change and Economic Performance*, Cambridge: Cambridge University Press.

North, Douglass C., 1990b, "A Transaction Cost Theory of Politics", *Journal of Theoretical Politics*, 2, 4, 355–367.

North, Douglass C., 1991, "Institutions", *The Journal of Economic Perspectives*, 5, 1, 97–112.

North, Douglass C., 1999, *Understanding the Process of Economic Growth*, Occasional Paper 106, London: Institute of Economic Affairs.

North, Douglass C., 2005, *Understanding the Process of Economic Growth*, Princeton, NJ: Princeton University Press.

OECD, 2008, *Investment Policy Review of China: Encouraging Responsible Business Conduct*, Paris: Organisation of Economic Cooperation and Development.

Oqubay, Arkebe and Justin Yifu Lin, 2019, *China-Africa and an Economic Transformation*, Oxford: Oxford University Press.

Orr, Ryan J. and W. Richard Scott, 2008, "Institutional Exceptions on Global Projects: A Process Model", *Journal of International Business Studies*, 39, 4, 562–588.

Ozawa, Terutomo, 2005, *Institutions, Industrial Upgrading and Economic Performance in Japan*, Cheltenham: Edward Elgar.

Peng, Mike W., 2003, "Institutional Transitions and Strategic Choices", *The Academy of Management Review*, 28, 2, 275–296.

Peng, Mike W., 2017, "Cultures, Institutions, and Strategic Choices: Toward an Institutional Perspective on Business Strategy", In: Martin J. Gannon and Karen L. Newman, eds., *The Blackwell Handbook of Cross-Cultural Management*, Oxford: Blackwell, 52–66.

Peng, Mike W. and Peggy Sue Heath, 1996, "The Growth of the Firm in Planned Economies in Transition: Institutions, Organizations, and Strategic Choice", *The Academy of Management Review*, 21, 2, 492–528.

Peng, Mike W. and Klaus Meyer, 2011, *International Business*, London: Cengage Learning.

Peng, Mike W., Denis Y.-L. Wang and Yi Jiang, 2008, "An Institution-Based View of International Business Strategy: A Focus on Emerging Economies", *Journal of International Business Studies*, 39, 5, 920–936.

Peterson, Barbara Bennett, 1994, "The Ming Voyages of Cheng Ho (Zheng He), 1371–1433", *The Great Circle*, 16, 1, 43–51.

Piat, Hugo Butcher, 2018, "China's New State Administration for Market Regulation", *China Briefing*, 11 October.

Ponte, Stefano, *et al.*, 2006, "To BEE or Not to BEE? South Africa's 'Black Economic Empowerment' (BEE), Corporate Governance and the State in the South", DIIS Working Paper No. 2006/27, Copenhagen: Danish Institute for International Studies.

Putnam, Robert D., 2000, *Bowling Alone: The Collapse and Revival of American Community*, New York: Simon and Schuster.

Pye, Lucian, 1992, *Chinese Commercial Negotiating Style*, New York: Quorum Books.

Qian, Jason and Anne Wu, 2007, "Playing the Blame Game in Africa", *International Herald Tribune*, 23 July.

Raine, Sarah, 2009, *China's Africa Challenges*, London: Routledge.

Rana, Mohammad B. and Glenn Morgan, 2019, "Twenty-Five Years of Business Systems Research and Lessons for International Business Studies", *International Business Review*, 28, 3, 513–532.

Raposo, Pedro, *et al.*, eds., 2018, *Routledge Handbook of Africa-Asia Relations*, London: Routledge.

Redding, Gordon and Michael A. Witt, 2008, "China's Business System and Its Future Trajectory", INSEAD Faculty and Research Working Paper 2008/59/EPS/EFE, Fontainebleau: Institut Européen d'Administration des Affaires.

Richardson, Peter, 1977, "The Recruiting of Chinese Indentured Labour for the South African Gold-Mines, 1903–1908", *The Journal of African History*, 18, 1, 85–108.

Rotberg, Robert I., ed., 2008, *China into Africa: Trade, Aid, and Influence*, Washington, DC: Brookings Institution.

Rugman, Alan M., 1981, *Inside the Multinationals: The Economics of Internal Markets*, New York: Columbia University Press.

Rugman, Alan M., 2008, "Do We Need a New Theory to Explain Emerging Market Multinationals", Conference Paper in: Five-Diamond International Conference Cycle: Conference 1: Thinking Outward: Global Players from Emerging Markets, 28–29 April, Columbia University, New York.

Rugman, Alan M. and Alain Verbeke, 2008, "Internalization Theory and Its Impact on the Field of International Business", In: Jean J. Boddewyn, ed., *International Business Scholarship: AIB Fellows on the First 50 Years and Beyond*, Bingley, UK: Emerald Group Publishing Limited, 155–174.

Rugman, Alan M., *et al.*, 2011, "Fifty Years of International Business Theory and Beyond", *Management International Review*, 51, 6, 755–786.

Sandry, Ron and Hannah Edinger, 2009, *Examining the South Africa-China Agricultural Trading Relationship*, Nordiska Afrikainstitutet Discussion Paper 42.

Sautet, Frederic, 2005, "The Role of Institutions in Entrepreneurship: Implications for Development Policy", *Mercatus Policy Series, Policy Primer*, No. 1, 1–14.

Schottenhammer, Angela, 2016, "China's Gate to the Indian Ocean: Iranian and Arab Long-Distance Traders", *Harvard Journal of Asiatic Studies*, 76, 1, 135–179.

Schwab, Klaus, 2019, *The Global Competitiveness Report, 2019*, Geneva: World Economic Forum.

Scott, John, 1991, *Social Network Analysis: A Handbook*, London: Sage Publications.

Scott, W. Richard, 1987, "The Adolescence of Institutional Theory", *Administrative Science Quarterly*, 32, 4, 493–511.

Scott, W. Richard, 2001, *Institutions and Organizations* (2nd Edition), London: Sage.

Scott, W. Richard, 2014, *Institutions and Organizations: Ideas, Interests and Identities* (4th Edition), Thousand Oaks, CA: Sage.

Sen, Tansen, 2016, "The Impact of Zheng He's Expeditions on Indian Ocean Interactions", *Bulletin of the School of Oriental and African Studies*, 79, 3, 609–636.

Seyfried, Christina, 2019, *Lecture 17: Filling the Void: China in Africa*, 21 November, www.youtube.com/watch?v=wMCF2eu1D0E.

Shinn, David H. and Joshua Eisenman, 2012, *China and Africa: A Century of Engagement*, Philadelphia: University of Pennsylvania Press.

Sigley, Gary, 2006, "Chinese Governmentalities: Government, Governance and the Socialist Market Economy", *Economy and Society*, 35, 4, 487–508.

Silva-Rêgo, Bernardo Frossard and Ariane Roder Figueira, 2019, "New Institutional Economics: Contributions to International Business Studies", *International Journal of Emerging Markets*, 14, 5, 1102–1123.

Smidt, Wolbert G.C., 2001, "A Chinese in the Nubian and Abyssinian Kingdoms (8th Century): The Visit of Du Huan to Molin-guo and Laobosa", *Arabian Humanities*, 9 (online).

Söderbaum, Peter, 1992, "Neoclassical and Institutional Approaches to Development and the Environment", *Ecological Economics*, 5, 2, 127–144.

Stahl, Anna Katharina, 2016, "China's Relations With Sub-Saharan Africa", *IAI Working Papers*, 16 (22), Rome: Istituto Affari Internazionali (IAI).

Story, Jonathan, 2004, "Strategies for China", In: Jonathan Story, ed., *The State of the Art: Handbook of Management* (3rd Edition), New Jersey: Prentice Hall, 127–140.

Story, Jonathan, 2010, *China Uncovered: What You Need to Know to Do Business in China*, London: Prentice Hall, Financial Times Series.

Su, Chenting and James E. Littlefield, 2001, "Entering Guanxi: A Business Ethical Dilemma in Mainland China?", *Journal of Business Ethics*, 33, 3, 199–210.

Suchman, Mark C., 1995, "Managing Legitimacy: Strategic and Institutional Approaches", *Academy of Management Journal*, 20, 3, 571–610.

Tang, Xiaoyang, 2020, *Coevolutionaty Pragmatism: Approaches and Impacts of China-Africa Economic Co-Operation*, Cambridge: Cambridge University Press.

Taylor, Ian, 1998, "China's Foreign Policy Towards Africa in the 1990s", *Journal of Modern African Studies*, 6, 3, 443–460.

Taylor, Ian and Tim Zajontz, 2020, "In a Fix: Africa's Place in the Belt and Road Initiative and the Reproduction of Dependency", *The South African Journal of International Affairs*, 27, 3, 277–295.

Tihanyi, Laszlo, Timothy M. Devinney and Torben Pedersen, eds., 2012, *Institutional Theory in International Business and Management: Volume 25*, Bingley, UK: Emerald, Advances in International Management.

Tilling, Matthew V., 2004, "Refinements to Legitimacy Theory in Social and Environmental Accounting", Flinders University School of Commerce 2004 Research Paper Series, No. 04–6.

Tomlinson, B.R., 2003, "What Was the Third World?", *Journal of Contemporary History*, 38, 2, 307–321.

Tsang, Eric W.K., 1998, "Can Guanxi Be a Source of Sustained Competitive Advantage for Doing Business in China?", *The Academy of Management Executive (1993–2005)*, 12, 2, 64–73.

Tung, Rosalie L. and Verner Worm, 1997, *The Importance of Networks (Guanxi) for European Companies in China*, Copenhagen: Copenhagen Business School.

UNCTAD, 2021, *World Investment Report*, Geneva: United Nations Conference on Trade and Development.

Voss, Hinrich, 2007, "The Foreign Direct Investment Behaviour of Chinese Firms: Does the 'New Institutional Theory' Approach Offer Explanatory Power?" PhD thesis, Leeds: University of Leeds.

Voss, Hinrich, 2011, *The Determinants of Chinese Outward Direct Investment*, Cheltenham: Edward Elgar, New Horizons in International Business Series.

Wade, Geoff, 2005, "The Zheng He Voyages: A Reassessment", *Journal of the Malaysian Branch of the Royal Asiatic Society*, 78, 1, 37–58.

Wang, Hongying, 2000, "Informal Institutions and Foreign Investment in China", *Pacific Review*, 13, 4, 525–556.

Welch, Catherine, Niina Nummela and Peter Liesch, 2016, "The Internationalization Process Model Revisited: An Agenda for Future Research", *Management International Review*, 56, 6, 783–804.

Western Cape Government, 2013, *Western Cape Government and South African Wines Excel in Beijing,* https://www.westerncape.gov.za/news/western-cape-government-and-south-african-wines-excel-beijing

Whitley, Richard, 1999, *Divergent Capitalisms: The Social Structuring and Change of Business Systems*, Oxford: Oxford University Press.

Whitley, Richard and Peer Hull Kristensen, 1996, *The Changing European Firm: Limits to Convergence*, London: Routledge.

Williamson, Claudia R., 2009, "Informal Institutions Rule: Institutional Arrangements and Economic Performance", *Public Choice*, 139, 3/4, 371–387.

Williamson, Oliver E., 2000, "The New Institutional Economics: Taking Stock, Looking Ahead", *Journal of Economic Literature*, 38, 3, 595–613.

Wolpe, Harold, 1972, "Capitalism and Cheap Labour-Power in South Africa: From Segregation to Apartheid", *Economy and Society*, 1, 4, 425–456.

Worden, Nigel, 2012, *The Making of Modern South Africa: Conquest, Apartheid, Democracy*, (5th Edition), Hoboken, NJ: John Wiley and Sons Inc.

Wu Zhong, 2006, "How Regionalism Is Holding Back China", *Asia Times*, 25 July.

Wyatt, Don, 2010, *The Blacks of Premodern China*, Philadelphia: University of Pennsylvania Press.

Xabadiya, Avuyile and Zhiquan Hu, 2019, "An Analysis of China-Africa Agricultural Co-Operation and Prospects of Belt and Road Initiative: A Case of South Africa", *International Journal of Academic Research in Business and Social Science*, 9, 2, 221–250.

Xiang, Yu, 2018, "China in Africa: Refiguring Centre-Periphery Media Dynamics", In: Daya Kishan Thussu, Hugo de Burgh and Anbin Shi, eds., *China's Media Go Global*, London: Routledge, 213–229.

Xu, Chenggang, 2011, "The Fundamental Institutions of China's Reforms and Development", *Journal of Economic Literature*, 49, 4, 1076–1151.

Yang, Juping, 2009, "Alexander the Great and the Emergence of the Silk Road", *The Silk Road*, 6/2, 15–22.

Yang, Mayfair Mei-hui, 1994, *Gifts, Favors, and Banquets: The Art of Social Relationships in China*, Ithaca, NY: Cornell University Press.

Young, Gary Keith, 2001, *Rome's Eastern Trade: International Commerce and Imperial Policy, 31 BC–AD 305*, London: Routledge.

Yu, George T., 1977, "China's Role in Africa", *Annals of the American Academy of Political and Social Science*, 432, 96–109.

Yu, George T., 1988, "Africa in Chinese Foreign Policy", *Asian Survey*, 28, 8, 849–862.

Zhang, Yi and Zigang Zhang, 2006, "Guanxi and Organisational Dynamics in China: A Link Between Individual and Organisational Levels", *Journal of Business Ethics*, 67, 4, 375–392.

Zimbauer, Dieter, 2001, "From Neo-Classical Economics to New Institutional Economics and Beyond: Prospects for an Interdisciplinary Research Programme?", Working Paper Series, Number 01–12, London: London School of Economics, Development Studies Institute.

Index

Note: Page numbers in *italics* indicate a figure on the corresponding page.

Abbasid Caliphate (visit) 2
additional payments, allowability (absence) 82
Africa: "China, Inc.," investment opportunities 9; Chinese outward forward direct investment (COFDI), increase 9; commodity bank, constraints 73; countries, debt burden (increase) 11; PRC, direct engagement 6
Africa Development Bank, China participation 9
African National Congress (ANC): economic policy, pursuit 21–22; foreign policy 21; institutional transition 22; open policy, adoption 21–22; policy guidelines 22; power 102; victory (1994) 21
Aksumite Kingdom, trading 2
Anglo-Boer War 4
Anglo-Chinese War (First Opium War) 17
Anshan, Li 2
anti-corruption measures 46
Anti-Japanese War 17
Anti-Monopoly Bureau, Price Supervision, Standardized Administration of China 39
apartheid regime (South Africa) 17–18; cessation 94; extremes 12
Arab merchant ships, impact 4
artefacts 32
autonomy, constriction 15–17

Bandung Conference 6–7
Bank of China (BOC) 67

basic institutions model 31
basic networks model 31
basic rules model 31
Battle of Talas 2
bedding in period 70
Beijing Foreign Enterprise Human Resources Service Co. (FESCO) assistance 71
Beijing, Intermediate Court 86
Beijing restaurant venture 64
Belt and Road Initiative (BRI) 10; Africa, involvement 11
Board to the Superior Court 87
Boer War 4
boundary-transgressors 48
Boxer Rebellion, impact 5
brand, control 61–62
Brazil, Russia, India, China and South Africa (BRICS) 12, 72; international institutional initiatives 78
bureaucratic hurdles, negotiation 68–69
business: activities, expansion/deepening 58; business-related social networks, building 102; consolidation/expansion 71–72; cooperation, initiation 73; dealings, lubrication 96–97; deal, mediation price 82; development cycle, closed cycle 53; development process 89; entity registration, rationale 82–83; failure, blame 64; government, relationship 87–97, *90*, *95*; initiative, networks (usage) 59–60; life-span 63; lubricant 44; partner control 79–87, *80*, *85*; record, success 63–64;

revenue, source 94; transforming processes, correspondence 53; transforming processes, types 52; visionary 99–100
business scenarios: description 52; firms, competitive advantages 53
business strategies: distinctiveness 79–80; flexibility, adoption 100; localisation 64–65; range 98
Business Studies 34

capacity building ("Eight Major Initiatives") 10
capital expenditure projects, fixed-term project contractors (usage) 93
Catalogues for Guidance on Foreign Investment Projects (CGFIP) 40
Central Asia, China access (severing) 3
central government, preferential policies 91
centralised polity 99
Chamber of Commerce, involvement 5
Chamber of Mines Labour Importation Agency, involvement 5
Chilean government, activity (contrast) 61
China: African states, commitment (reaffirmation) 9–10; autonomy, constriction 15–17; bureaucratic/administrative channels, navigation 50; comparative transitions 11–12, *13–14*; connection, mediation 65–66; corruption, crackdown 49; customers, attraction 78; domestic market, potential 37; economic growth 103; economic reform process, macro-control 38; economic transition 11; Egypt, diplomatic relations 7; empire, republic transition 17; energy sector market business strategies, analysis 87–97, *90, 95*; enterprise, development 84; financial market business strategies, analysis 66–79, *67, 70, 74*; firms, rules (application) 50–51; formal institutional environment, negotiation (success) 83; formal institutions 37–39; General Administration of Customs (GACC) 37, 39; generic umbrella

45; globalisation 21–25; "Go-Out" (Go Global) policy (1999) 9; *guanxi* system, imperatives 45; informal institutions 44–51; institutional environment 36–39; institutional evolution, catching-up process 25; insurance business opportunity 69; international re-connection (1948–1994) 17–25; investment, restricted catalogue 40–41; isolationism 3–4; joint ventures 36; language, acceptance 62; level business playing field 36–37; local helping hand, importance 63–64; machinery market business strategies, analysis 79–87, *80, 85*; macro-level institutions 37; meso-level institutions 41; micro-level institutions 41, 43–44; mind-set, requirement 101; Ministry of Commerce (MOFCOM) 37, 38; National Development and Reform Commission (NDRC) 38; open-door policy (1949–1994) 19–20; open doors 22, 25, 99; overproduction/pollution/worker safety fear, local governments (perspective) 43; partners, lawsuits 86; People's Bank of China (PBC) 37, 40–51; personal networks, problems 81–82; planned economy, change 19–20; political economy, survival 20; reform process, by-product 43; seasonal festivals 49; self-reliance (1948–1994) 17–25; socio-cultural landscape, negotiation 44–45; South African firms, business strategies (investigation) 98; South African wineries, entry 58; South-South cooperation (1994–present) 21–25; State Administration for Foreign Exchange (SAFE) 37, 39; State Administration for Industry and Commerce (SAIC) 37; State Administration for Market Regulation (SAMR) 38–39; State Administration for Taxation (SAT) 37, 39; State Council of China (Central People's Government) 37; State-owned Assets Supervision and Administration Commission of the

State Council (SASAC) 39; state-owned investment company, contract 72; strongman politics 43; trade agreement, finalisation 60; trade volumes, increase 94

China/Africa: connectivity, increase 4; relations, history 1–6

"China and Africa: Toward an Even Strong Community with a Shared Future through Win-Win Cooperation" 10

China Banking and Insurance and Regulatory Commission (CBIRC) 40, 67

China Banking Regulatory Commission (CBRC) 40–51; formal approval, obtaining 75

China Development Bank 10

"China, Inc.," investment opportunities 9

China Insurance Regulatory Commission (CIRC) 40–51; five-year rep office requirement 69

China Securities Regulatory Commission (CSRC) 40–51

China/South Africa: contrast 19–20; political/economic relations, institutional transition viewpoint 11–25

China team, building 71

Chinese business: consolidation/expansion 71; interactions, understanding 29; operation methods 51; opportunities 78; strategies, analysis *59*, 59–65, *63*; success, sensitivity 60–61; withdrawal 88

Chinese market: commodity bank entry, constraints 73; entry mode 51; entry, timing 101; expansion strategy 58; foreign company entry, difficulty 20; inbound FDI 39; market-based financial incentives 19; path, success 61; penetration/operation, business approach 70–71; South African business firms, engagement 98; unpredictability, South African firm (awareness) 104

Chinese outward forward direct investment (COFDI), increase 9

Chinese state-owned enterprises (SOEs) 19, 74, 83; assigning 89–90;

central/regional governments, attachment 91–92; clients, identification 94; collaboration 74; management 39; reform 9; shareholders, involvement 76

Civil War (Kuomintang/Communist Party) 17

coal-to-liquid (CTL) technology 87, 89

Cold War: privations 18; Sino-African relations 6–8, 12

collaboration mode, problems 88

colonialism, exit 6

commissions, usage 82

commodity trading 72–732

Commonwealth Conference 10

communication: enhancement 96; problems, ease 92

Communist Party of China (CPC): durability 19–20; establishment 17; monopoly position 20; power 6; ruling party 19

company: business entity registration, rationale 82–83; company-specific competitive advantage 68; customer base, maintenance 47; involvement, scale (institutionalised limits) 66–67; president replacement 92

Comparative Institutionalism (CI) 30; emanation 32

consolidation, facilitation 60

contextual intuition, deployment 64–65

contextual problems, navigation 64

co-operation project, NDRC termination 88

corporate business objective 35

corruption, crackdown 49

country specific advantages (CSAs) 54–55, 91, 105

COVID-19 pandemic, impact 10

cross-border mergers and acquisitions (M&As) 72–73

cultural context, difference 81

cultural familiarity, building 51

Cultural Revolution, cessation 8, 22, 25

customer base, maintenance 47

debt-trap diplomacy 11

Deng, Xiaoping 43; power 8; reforms (1978) 19, 22, 25

documentary procedures 66

domestic firms, survival 20
domestic transition process, international market engagement (connections) 11–12
due diligence, usage 64–65
Du, Huan 2

East Africa, Indians (arrival) 5
economic dynamics/efficiency, institutions (role) 32–33
"Eight Major Initiatives" 10
"Eight Principles of Economic and Technical Aid" (China) 7
Electricity Supply Commission (ESCOM) 16
Electricity Supply Commission (Eskom) 18
Eleventh Party Congress of the Communist Party, domestic reforms 8
emerging country markets, IB studies interest 27
Emigration Convention Between the United Kingdom and China Respecting the Employment of Chinese Labour in the British Colonies and Protectorates, signing 5
Emperor Yong-Le (boat-building/ navigation) 3
employees: exchanges, understanding/ learning opportunity 76; full-time employees, usage 93
energy sector: business strategies, analysis 87–97, *90*, *95*; government support, importance 90
environmental perspective 325
equity shareholdings, limitation 66
established regulations, absence 68
European African Summit 10
Export-Import Bank of China 10
export trade, scope (enhancement) 38
externalisation 92; process 60, 71–72, 92–93

failure/success, contrast 57–65
feasibility study, results 92
financial capital, injection 75
financial market business strategies, analysis 66–79, *67*, *70*, *74*
financial markets 65–79

firms: firm-level competitive advantages 54; firm-level (micro) institutions, influences 33; firm-resource-oriented business scenarios 53; personality of the firm 101; resources, utilisation 67; transforming process 54
firm-specific advantages (FSAs) 54–55, 91–92, 99, 105
First Opium War 17
five-year rep office, CIRC requirement 69
fixed-term project contractors, usage 93
foreign corporations, managers (institution perception) 20
foreign direct investment (FDI): flows, statistical analysis (improvement) 28; inbound FDI (China) 39; South African FDI, multi-dimensional institutional analysis 36
foreign dominance, freedom 12
foreign firms: channel 409; *guanxi* (relationship) 50–51
foreign insurance, premium income (increase) 72
foreign-investing firms, class types 57
foreign investment, mature destination 101
foreign market location, concern 99
foreign-owned firms, rules (application) 50–51
foreign personal insurance institutions, direct investment 72
formal economic institutions, political orchestration 41
formal institutional contact 104
formal institutions (China) 37–39
formal institutions, rule-based perspective 34
formal institutions, structure (People's Republic of China) *42*
formal quasi-formal institutional practices 30
Forum on China-Africa Cooperation (FOCAC) 9–11
four-stage transforming process 106
Fourteenth Party Congress (1992) 22, 25
Franco-African Summit 10
Free Trade Agreement, establishment 61

ganqing 46
gas-to-liquid (GTL) technology 87

General Administration of Customs (GACC) (China) 37, 39
gift-giving: constraints 46; *guanxi* currency 49; prominence 48
globalisation (1994–present) 21–25
Going Global strategy (PRC) 10
going local, notion (importance) 56
goodwill, underwriting 46
government: approval, prospects (increase) 92; business, relationship 87–97, *90*, *95*; institutional approvals (legitimation), application 75; relationships 93; systems, effectiveness 29
Great Depression (1929) 16
Great Proletarian Cultural Revolution 7
green development ("Eight Major Initiatives") 10
Guangzhou, Persian community (development) 2
guanxi 81; artefactual *guanxi* 45; building 51; character/functionality, permutations 49; defining 44–45; ethics, debate 48; foreign firms, relationship 50–51; gift-giving currency 49; historical/cultural roots 50; importance 47–58; institutional elements 49; institutionalisation process 48–50; institution, weakening (absence) 50; negative/positive connotations 48; networks, influencers 46; networks, spatial mobility (interference) 50; networks, usage 47; origin 45–47; *sheng-ren guanxi* 51; system, imperatives 45; trust, importance 49; vital products 46

Han Dynasty, China/Africa connections 1
healthcare ("Eight Major Initiatives") 10
health insurance products/services, expertise/experience 68
heavy machinery demand (increase), capitalisation position 79
higher-echelon stakeholders, connections 92
higher-level government networks, channel 89–90
higher-level government officials, mediating conduit 93

higher-level institutional environment, company path 80
higher-level institutions, formal/informal networking 84–85
higher-level network connections, usage 59–60
high-level institutional arrangement 74
high-level institutional connections, impact 67–68
high-profile connections, nurturing/maintenance 75
Hong Kong: airport project 84; foreign capital controls, reduction 82–83; sales office, Chinese staff (employment) 95; taxation system (ease) 82–83
Hong Kong Special Administrative Region (SAR) 82–83
human resources 35
hybrid socialist-neoliberal economy (China) 25

imperialism, exit 6
inbound foreign investment 48
indigenous state-owned companies, high-profile connections 75
Industrial Development Corporation (IDC) 18
industrialisation (South Africa) 15
industrial promotion ("Eight Major Initiatives") 10
in-firm management capacity, improvement 38
informal business practices, institutionalisation 48
informal institutional arrangements, trust (importance) 35
informal institutional channels, usage 101
informal institutional contact 104
informal institutional practices 43
informal institutional rules of the game 82–83
informal institutions: defining 35; formalisation, absence 34; manifestations 35; norm-based perspective 34
informal institutions (China) 44–51
informal quasi-formal institutional practices 30

infrastructure connectivity ("Eight Major Initiatives") 10
infrastructure extraction projects 77
institutional architecture, uniformity 43
institutional carriers 32
institutional connectivity 100
institutional context, difference 81
institutional environments 27; difficulty 63; navigation 96–97
institutional factors 35
institutional initiatives (South Africa) *23–24*
institutional landscape, ambiguity 44
institutional model 27
institutional model analysis 57; case studies 57
institutional model, three-dimensional (3D) institutional model *52*, 52–56
institutional practice, structural layers 36
institution-based strategies, role 31
institutions: defining 33; normative perspective 34; operationalisation, institutional approach 33–36; organisations, contrast 30–31; rules of the game 30–31
institution, term (usage) 106
insurance industry, company operation 69
intangible equities 35
intellectual property (IP): concern 103–104; improvement 66; infringements 84–85; legal protection, regulation 85; protection 91, 103–104; protection reform process 87; regulation/enforcement risks 85
intellectual property rights (IPR): infringements 84, 86; regulatory/supervisory systems, reform 87
intention to cooperate, signing 88
intermediary (meso-level) institutions, links 33
internal/external institutional interfaces 52
internalisation: advantages 91; process 80
internal power relations 35
international business (IB) experience, impact 84
international business (IB) interactions, third wave 27
international business (IB) pitfall 98–99
international business (IB) studies: contributions 104–105; findings

98–101; institutional approach 30–33; institutional perspective 28–36; research suggestions 106–107
international business (IB) theories, explanations 29
international institutional initiatives 78
internationalisation, phases 12
Internationalisation Theory 28
international re-connection (1948–1994) 17–25
International Relations (IR), issues 27
international trading principles, impact 82
interpersonal networks, usage 96
Investment promotion agencies (IPA), regulatory guidance 38
investments, making 35
IPE 34
Iron and Steel Industrial Corporation (ISCOR) 16

Jansson, Han 106
Jin Dynasty conquerors, impact 3
Jingxingji (travel tales) 2
Johannesburg Stock Exchange (JSE): listing 65, 76, 83; value 18
joint capital arrangements, involvement 51
joint venture (JV): establishment 68; model, avoidance 86; partner, meeting 58; setup 65
joint ventures, involvement 51

King Mu travels (Zhou Dynasty) 1
knowledge sources 96–97

Labour Importation Ordinance, impact 5
late British Colonial era (South Africa) 15–17
lease renewal, influence (inability) 65
Lee, Kwan Yew 47
Legislative Council of South Africa, involvement 5
legitimation: application 75; function, defining 55; process 55, 66
leverage, increase 92–93
life insurance sub-sector, contract (obtaining) 72
Likan (Alexandria, claim) 1
loan default, partner reluctance 47

local authorities, sub-regulations/rules 41
local government officials/partners, relationships (strengthening) 89
local helping hand, importance 63–64
local institutional environment, sensitivity 60–61
local intelligence, usage 64–65
localisation 78; facilitation 81
localisation process 75; Chinese partner assistance 68–69
local-level institutions, state-level institutions (relationship lubrication) 41
local market dominance, importance 100
local partner, interaction (advantage) 78
local Port Authority, special arrangements 96
location, importance (analysis) 103
London Stock Exchange (LSE), listing 83
long-term franchise value, impact 76
lubrication, impact 48

machinery: distribution group 79; supply 83–84
machinery market 79–87, *80*, *85*; business strategies, analysis 79–87, *80*, *85*
macro-level external institutions, comparison 35
macro-level (state-level) factors, analysis consistency (absence) 31
macro-level institutions: influences 33; micro-level institutions, gap 31; permutations 52
macro-level institutions (China) 37
macro structure, providing 33
management structure/nature 35
Mandarin (language): acceptance 62; usage 80
Mandela, Nelson 21
Mao, Zedong 43; death 8; peasant farmer focus 17
market-based financial incentives (China) 19
market economy 100
market entry: facilitation 60; progress, smoothing 80
marketing: approach 62; mechanism, efficiency 64
market intelligence, usage 70

Memorandum of Understanding (MoU), basis 77
mergers and acquisitions (M&As) 72–73
meso-level external institutions, creation 36
meso-level institutions: permutations 52; series, creation 31
meso-level institutions (China) 41
micro institutional system 102
micro-level (firm-level) factors, analysis consistency (absence) 31
micro-level institutions: environments 53; macro-level institutions, gap 31
micro-level institutions (China) 41, 43–44
Mid-Autumn Festival (Chinese festival) 49
Middle Eastern partner, approach 64
mineral revolution (South Africa) 15–17
Ming Dynasty: porcelain, discovery 3; relations, stasis 6
Ministry of Commerce (MOFCOM) (China) 37, 38
Ministry of Ecology and Environment project, approval 89
multi-national corporations (MNCs): business activities 29–30; development 105; foreign investment activities 28; guidance 56; locational choices, challenge 56; penetration/operation 36
mutual understanding, enhancement 96

National Development and Reform Commission (NDRC) (China) 37, 38, 41, 43, 88
National Party/Labour Party, coalition (1924) (South Africa) 16
National People's Congress (NPC), supreme power 37
natural resources 38
Naughton, Barry 19
networks: formal/informal networking 84–85; interpersonal networks, usage 96; network-building 35; network-building, deprioritisation 92–93; network-opportunity mobilisation 60; network-oriented opportunity,

company response 67–68; operational effectiveness, serendipity (role) 35; opportunity 72; structure, thinness 54
New Institutional Economics (NIE) 30, 31; NOI, contrast 32
New Organizational Institutionalism (NOI) 30; IB scholar engagement 31–32; NIE, contrast 32
New Year (Chinese festival) 49
niche market, identification 71
non-profit entity, presence 69
norms-ignorers 48
North China, co-operation project (survival) 89
North, Douglass 30, 31, 33

OLI paradigm 55
open-door policy (1949–1994) (China) 19–20
organisations, institutions (contrast) 30–31
outcomes, differences 65–79
Overseas Chinese in Africa, The (Anshan) 2
overseas foreign direct investment (OFDI) 102, 106

parastatal enterprises 18
Patent Reexamination Board (SIPO) 86
patronage, impact 60
patron-clientship 45
pax Ming, establishment 3
peace ("Eight Major Initiatives") 10
Peng, Mike 106
people, relations/interactions (bridging) 54
People's Bank of China (PBC) 37, 40–51
People's Republic of China (PRC): Africa, direct engagement 6; Africa policy, reduction 7; appearance 8; formal institutions, structure *42*; Going Global strategy 10; South Africa, formal relations 28; South Africa, Free Trade Agreement (establishment) 61
people-to-people exchange ("Eight Major Initiatives") 10
personal interconnections/networks 53

personality of the firm 101
personal networks, importance 60
personal networks, usage 59–60; problems 81–82
personal recommendation, impact 71
Phosphate Development Corporation (Foskor) 18
planned economy, change (China) 19–20
policy context, impact 67
political patronage 19–20
post-apartheid era (South Africa) 21–22
private sector, size (increase) 50
privatisation 90
products/service, promotion (marketing approach) 62
promotion mechanism, efficiency 64

Qing Dynasty: diplomatic relations, stasis 6; formal diplomatic relations, severing 4

reciprocity, impact 34–35
relational systems 32
relationship-building, importance 93–94
renqing 49
Representative Office 51; establishment 71, 72, 75
Republic of China, PRC replacement 8
resource: extraction projects 77; resource-oriented experience 64
retail banking 76
"right" people, invitation 60
routines 32
rule-breakers 48
rules-based economy 99
rules-based institutional setting, evolution 96–97
rules of the game 30, 31, 33, 45; informal institutional rules of the game 82–83; rigidity 104–105

SAB Miller, internationalised South African label 100
Scott, Richard 31–32
seaport project, joint project (opportunity) 96
security ("Eight Major Initiatives") 10
self-reliance (1948–1994) 17–25

serendipity, impact 35
Seven Voyages of Admiral Zheng He 1, 3–4
shareholders: interests, threat 75; sustainable returns, generation 76
sheng-ren guanxi 51
Sigley, Gary 25
Silk Road 1, 10
Singapore, restaurant opening 61; problems 62
Sino-African business co-operation, Chinese preferential policies 81
Sino-African political relations 25
Sino-African relations: Cold War (1950s–1970s) 6–8; development 6–11; rekindling 7–8; severing 4; Sino-Africa New Age (21st century) 9–11; transitional era (1970s–1990s) 8–10
Sino-Soviet struggle, Africa (battleground) 7–8
social capital: bridging 47; usage 34
social/familial/territorial networks 35
social interaction/investment, usage 45–46
socialist market economy (China) 22, 25, 99
social systems 45
Song Dynasty, trade connections 2–3
South Africa: apartheid regime 17–18; autonomy, constriction 15–17; banks, involvement 72; business activities, expansion/deepening 58; business, comparison 101–104; business expansion/consolidation 18; business interactions, understanding 29; Chinese banks, presence 78; Chinese migration, occurrence 5–6; comparative transitions 11–12, *13–14*; economic environment, balance/dynamism 21–22; expatriates, subsidiaries management/ communications 100; FDI, multidimensional institutional analysis 36; financial acquisition deal 73; globalisation 21–25; gold, economic cushion 16; gold ore/capital flight 4; gold resources 15; industrialisation 15; institutional framework, British institutions (association)

16–17; institutional initiatives *23–24*; institutional transitions 16–17; insurance company, operation 69; insurance products, license 69–70; international re-connection (1948–1994) 17–25; investment, Chinese institutional environment 36–39; late British Colonial era 15–17; mineral revolution 15–17; National Party (NP)/Labour Party, coalition (1924) 16; National Party (NP), victory (1948) 17; natural resources, advantages 15; parastatal enterprises 18; political control, British seizure 15; political institutional environments 18; populations/races, conflicts 15; post-apartheid era 21–22; PRC, formal relations 28; principles, meeting 21; racial segregation, system 17; restaurant chain, business plan 61; self-reliance (1948–1994) 17–25; self-sufficiency, strengthening 15; SOEs, mismanagement 22; South-South cooperation (1994–present) 21–25; Taiwan, diplomatic relationship 95; West, ally 12; wineries, guidance 57–58
South Africa-China Bi-National Commission 12
South Africa iron ore, production 93
South African Coal, Oil and Gas Corporation (SASOL) 18
South African Communist Party, Chinese Communist Party (contact, maintenance) 12
South African firms: investigation, case studies (usage) 103–104; local market dominance, importance 100; "no turning back" motivation 99; overseas foreign direct investment (OFDI) 102, 106
South African Iron and Steel Corporation (Iscor) 18
South African Reserve Bank, formal approval (obtaining) 75
Southeast Asia, immigration policies 5
Southern Oil Exploration Corporation (Soekor) 18
South-South cooperation (1994–present) 21–25

Special Administrative Region (SAR) 82–83
Spring Festival (Chinese festival) 49
standardised legal procedures, absence 68
State Administration for Foreign Exchange (SAFE) (China) 39
State Administration for Industry and Commerce (SAIC) 37, 39
State Administration for Market Regulation (SAMR) (China) 38–39
State Administration for Taxation (SAT) (China) 37, 39
State Council Institutional Reform Program, SAMR creation 39
State Council of China (Central People's Government) (China) 37
State Council Office for Restructuring the Economic System (SCORES) 38
State Development Planning Commission (SDPC) 38
State Economic and Trade Commission (SETC) 38
state financial sector policies/ regulations, control 74
State Intellectual Property Office (SIPO) 39, 86
state-level institutions: analysis 32; local-level institutions, relationship (lubrication) 41
State-owned Assets Supervision and Administration Commission of the State Council (SASAC) (China) 39
state-owned enterprises (SOEs) 19; connections, formation 80–81; counterclaim 86; legal process interference 86; maintenance 87–88; management 39; mismanagement (ANC) 22; reform (China) 9
strategic alliance 75–76
strategic business partnership, announcement 73
strategic co-operation agreement 76; establishment 77
strategic international business development 94
strategies, differences 65–79
Structural Adjustment Programmes 8–9

sub-national (meso-level) institutions, emphasis 32
success/failure, contrast 57–65
symbolic systems 32

Taiwan: harm 6–7; South Africa, diplomatic relationship 95
Taiwan (ROC), growth 7
Tang Dynasty, China/Africa connectivity (increase) 4
targets, differences 65–79
technology: absorption 85; commercialisation 87–88; reliance 85; transfer 38
third-party company, products purchase 82
three-dimensional (3D) institutional model *52*, 52–56; analysis 57; building blocks, formation 106; case studies 57; China, business strategies (analysis) *59*, 59–65, *63*; energy sector market business strategies, analysis 87–97, *90*, *95*; financial market business strategies, analysis 66–79, *67*, *70*, *74*; machinery market business strategies, analysis 79–87, *80*, *85*; rationale 105
three pillars framework 32
Tiananmen Square (1989), suppression 19
Tokyo International Conference on African Development 10
totalitarianism, extremes 12
trade facilitation ("Eight Major Initiatives") 10
transmission processes 54–55
triad economies, historical association 28
trust: building 46; importance 35, 49

uncertainties, reduction 31, 53
underdevelopment, exit 6
unethical actors, impact 48
upper-level institutional players, business-related social networks (building) 102
upper-level institutional structure, legitimation process 55

upper-level institutions, VIP contacts 80–81
Uppsala Model, decision-making 28
US African Growth and Opportunity Act 10

value system 35

Western capitalism, domination 8–9
Western markets, access 65
Wholly-Owned Foreign Enterprise (WOFE): business venture, setup 76; establishment 61–62, 75, 79, 84; initiation 69; model, usage 64; setup 86; ventures, establishment 79
Williamson, Oliver 30

Witwatersrand Basin in the Transvaal (Zuid-Afrikaansche Republiek) 4
World Trade Organization (WTO), China (accession) 25, 36, 41, 50

Xi, Jinping 10, 49

yijian rugu 46
Yuan Dynasty: Indian Ocean trade 4; trade connections 2–3

Zhang, Qian 1
Zhao, Ziyang (Africa visit) 9
Zheng, He (Seven Voyages) 1, 3–4
Zhou Dynasty, King Mu (travels) 1
Zhou, En'lai (African visits) 7
Zhu, Rongji 88

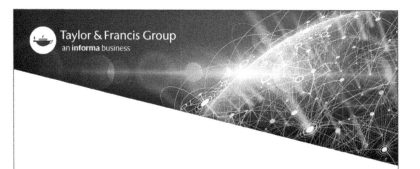

www.ingramcontent.com/pod-product-compliance
Ingram Content Group UK Ltd.
Pitfield, Milton Keynes, MK11 3LW, UK
UKHW020438010325
455677UK00030B/1197